Mennonite Literary Voices

Past and Present

Mennonite Literary Voices

Past and Present

by Al Reimer

Bethel College
North Newton, Kansas
1993

Wedel Series logo by Angela Goering Miller
Copyright © 1993 by Al Reimer
Published by Bethel College
Printed and distributed by Pandora Press

Library of Congress Catalog number 93-70395

ISBN-13: 978-0963016027

Cornelius H. Wedel Historical Series

Contents

Introduction

In October 1991 Al Reimer, Professor Emeritus of English at the University of Winnipeg, presented the fortieth series in the Menno Simons Lectureship at Bethel College in Kansas. Those lectures, "Mennonite Literary Voices Past and Present," were the basis for this book.

Reimer serves as co-editor of *Journal of Mennonite Studies*, as senior editor for Mennonite Literary Society in Winnipeg, as consulting editor for *Mennonite Quarterly Review*, and was editor of *Mennonite Mirror* in Winnipeg from 1978 to 1987. He is the author of *My Harp is Turned to Mourning*, a Russian Mennonite historical novel, and has translated and edited two Russian Mennonite novels: *A Russian Dance of Death* and *No Strangers in Exile*. He has edited the Low German works of Arnold Dyck in two volumes and has co-edited five books in the fields of Mennonite literature and the Low German language.

Chapter two of this volume appeared, in slightly altered form, in *Journal of Mennonite Studies*, Vol. 10, 1992, pp. 20-26. Chapter three was in *Mennonite Life*, March 1992, pp. 20-26.

Chapter 1

Where Did the Voices Come From?

"In the beginning was the Word":
Anabaptist Writing
and the Russian–Mennonite Tradition

In his 1976 Menno Simons lectures *Mennonite Identity and Literary Art*, John L. Ruth argued eloquently for a Mennonite literature that would grow out of the Anabaptist Mennonite imperative of faith and belief, a literature coming directly from "that unique center of covenant-conviction where we stand,"[1] a literature that would "achieve a creative balance between critique and advocacy."[2] His lectures were hortatory, prescriptive, theoretically persuasive and useful as guides. I shall have more to say about them in my final chapter. They were, however, written at a time when Mennonite literature was appearing only sporadically in North America, the individual voices largely lost in a wilderness of Mennonite indifference to the arts, when it wasn't outright hostility. Ruth mentioned the names of only two Mennonite writers with approval: Rudy Wiebe and Warren Kliewer.

In the intervening years the Mennonite literary scene has changed dramatically. Today we have a fresh, exciting, rapidly growing body of Mennonite writing no longer restricted to a few isolated voices but grown to a veritable chorus, especially in Canada. Its focal point is Winnipeg, where an enterprising group of Mennonite writers is adding depth and lustre to Mennonite ethnoculture and to Canadian literature as a whole. This vigorous new writing calls for a preliminary appraisal, for some observations and judgments about its quality and range, about what these often provocative literary voices have to say to the Mennonite community about Mennonite experience. And I want to begin by tracing the origins of a Mennonite literary tradition, if indeed one exists.

What exactly is Mennonite writing? How do we define it? What and whom do we include, what and whom do we exclude from consideration? Is there, in fact, one homogeneous kind of Mennonite writing, or are there various kinds which may or may

---

[1]John L. Ruth, *Mennonite Identity and Literary Art* (Scottdale: Herald Press, 1978), 13.
[2]Ibid., 63.

not share enough family characteristics to warrant being called Mennonite? What about earlier Dutch and German writers of Mennonite background who joined the cultural mainstream—from the poet Joost van den Vondel in seventeenth-century Holland, say, to playwright Hermann Sudermann in nineteenth-century Germany—is their work outside the sphere of what we call Mennonite writing? How different is Swiss-Mennonite writing (what there is of it) from the Russian-Mennonite kind (of which there is considerably more)? John Ruth talked about Mennonite literary art mainly in terms of his American Swiss-Mennonite background. My Canadian-Mennonite heritage being that of the Dutch-Prussian-Russian group, I am drawn to the literature of that tradition. And since most of the serious Mennonite writing in Canada (and to a lesser extent in the U.S.) continues to come from writers bred in that particular Mennonite ethos, I have all the more reason to make it my main focus in this book.

I prefer to view "Mennonite" writing through a wide-angle lens which includes in its focus the work of writers who spent at least their formative years in a Mennonite milieu—family and/or community and/or church—regardless of whether they now consider themselves "Mennonite" in a religious sense, or in a purely ethnic sense, or in both senses, or in neither sense. I have not chosen this broad approach to Mennonite writing arbitrarily, nor out of frustration with the difficulty of finding a more precise, less inclusive definition that would be acceptable to the more conservative Mennonite reader. Rather, I would argue that some of the most exciting and challenging "Mennonite" writing is coming from the writers who are most disenchanted with their Mennonite world, whose motives are anger and outrage, who write to expose it, to reject it, or who endeavor to write themselves out of their Mennonite experience once and for all. I would exclude from my purview only those writers who have passed over into the mainstream without a qualm or a quiver or a backward glance at whatever Mennonite background or experience they could lay claim to if they really cared. Such literary amnesiacs suffer from a self-inflicted ethnic lobotomy that deserves our pity because it denies them access to the very well-springs of their being.

In this opening chapter, then, I want to look ahead into the past for early signs of a Mennonite literary imagination and style in Anabaptist writings and bring our story forward to the pivotal generation of Russian-Mennonite emigré writers that established the beginnings of a German-Mennonite literary tradition in North

America from the 1920s through the 1950s, after which it was swamped by a rising tide of writing in English.[3] As we might expect, the roots of the Mennonite literary imagination are to be found in radical Anabaptist-Mennonite religious experience. Moreover, that early spiritual bias in Mennonite literature has never been entirely lost, and is alive today even among the more dissident Mennonite writers, perhaps especially among them in its more radical form. As the Canadian writer and critic Magdalene Redekop has stated: "The writers who are on the periphery, challenging the very idea of being Mennonite, may paradoxically be the most true to the spirit of Reformation dissenters."[4] This is a theme I shall be coming back to in later chapters.

The notion that all art, including literature, draws much of its inspiration and potency from religious belief has a long and honorable history in Western culture. The noted Canadian critic Northrop Frye has done as much as any modern thinker to reveal the symbiotic relationship between the Bible and Western literature. In *Words With Power*, his final book, he explains that both religion and literature have their origins in a species of myth, i.e. universal stories about gods and their acts designed to explain the otherwise inexplicable conundrums and complexities of human existence. As we know, in literary criticism and related disciplines the term myth (from Greek *mythos*, meaning literally story) denotes the very opposite of its debased common meaning as unreal, fallacious, or non-existent. In Jungian terms, myths are archetypal patterns in human consciousness, original revelations of the preconscious psyche. The universal images or symbols of the great myths rise spontaneously from the collective unconscious as a response to the instinctual needs of the human psyche. The psychotherapist Rollo May claims that "Myths are

---

[3]Over the centuries Mennonite literary voices have suffered from their inability to find an authentic literary language. Dutch was gradually lost to the Mennonites after they moved to the Vistula delta in the 16th century, although assimilated Mennonites who remained in Holland contributed importantly to Dutch literature. In Russia, Low German remained only a spoken vernacular while High German, the church language, never became the language of everyday experience enough to qualify as a true literary language. And historical circumstances prevented Russian from becoming the dominant language, as English has become for North American Mennonites.

[4]Magdalene Redekop, *Prairie Fire: A Special Issue on Canadian Mennonite Writing* 11 (summer 1990): 46.

narrative patterns that give significance to our lives."[5] As such, the great universal myths cut across all cultural, linguistic, and historical barriers. The mythic pattern of the Bible includes the great myths of creation, the fall, exodus and migration, the apocalypse and final redemption to form the full cycle of human destiny. The concept of myth does not deny historicity or historical causes; it simply transcends time-space limitations.[6]

When a mythology, that is, a collection of related myths, is no longer accepted as a religion, it passes over into literature, as happened with ancient Greek, Roman, and Norse mythologies. A mythology retaining its religious credibility is typically ritualized and institutionalized as a religious ideology, according to Frye, and is thus adapted to "structures of social authority,"[7] as in the case of the Christian religion. But in this process of transformation, argues Frye, "Accepted myths soon cease to function as myths: they are asserted to be historical facts or descriptive accounts of what really happened."[8] The favored myths are "demythologized" from their symbolically charged mythic language by being translated into whatever rhetoric the ideology deems as authoritative and convincing.[9] Thus, the open-ended imaginative constructs of myth become the "solidified dogma" (Frye's term) of the controlling ideology.[10]

Once myth has been converted into dogma it is accepted unconditionally and regarded as sacrosanct. All other myths are then branded as "heretical, morbid, unreal or evil," Frye states, and the received "truth" of the approved "mythological canon" is no longer open to question.[11] In the case of Christianity this is what happened to the Bible. How it has been read and interpreted depended on whatever ideologically formulated doctrine was brought to bear on it, whether Catholic or Protestant. As Frye puts it: "An open Bible was one of the central issues of the Reformation, but a Calvinist, for example, read not the Bible but the Bible through Calvin's interpretation of the

[5]Rollo May, *The Cry for Myth* (New York: W. W. Norton & Company, 1991), 15.

[6]Ibid., 27.

[7]Northrop Frye, *Words With Power: Being a Second Study of the Bible and Literature* (Markham: Viking, 1990), 46.

[8]Ibid., 34.

[9]Ibid., 33.

[10]Ibid., 22.

[11]Ibid., 24.

Bible."[12] The same would hold true for the Anabaptists. In *Martyrs Mirror* we find a remarkable unanimity of scriptural interpretation among the martyrs as they assert the "literal" truths of the Bible.

The Anabaptist attempt to demythologize the Bible into a divinely inspired document in which doctrine and history were clearly and unambiguously rendered as the literal truth, was not without its inherent problems, however. A *written* God, offering the Word in the language of everyday life, as opposed to the *iconic* God of the Catholic tradition, is completely internalized and does not, like the iconic art, iconic chanting, and symbolic architecture of Catholicism, divert attention from the central concern of the Word. The problem is that the written word is itself a symbol system of a symbol system and so twice removed from reality. Which means, of course, that there are problems of interpretation inherent in language itself and in how it is used, problems that iconic church art tries to circumvent with a direct appeal to the senses. We know, for example, that while Menno himself favored the simplest, most literal interpretation of Scripture, his influential Dutch colleague Dirk Phillips favored the more flexible allegorical method inherited from the medieval church.[13]

Given the essential ambiguity of language itself, it is all the more necessary for a religious ideology to control language and meaning. The sacred code must prevail over the common code of meaning. It simply cannot afford the free play of the imagination and the kind of creative impulse demanded by open-ended literary myth. That would explain why freely invented literary forms have been so consistently branded in the Anabaptist-Mennonite tradition as at best frivolous, at worst as "lies" inspired by Satan. Since biblical myths were not lies but the historical "truth," only the hermeneutical myths attached to them were acceptable as further elaborations of the truth. And they required—in stark contrast to the biblical myths themselves—a clear, simple, straightforward style scraped clean (or almost clean) of tropes and other verbal ornamentation so that it would not be a meretricious literary language or a casuistical rhetoric to "confuse," but a plain literal language of truth and life for the common man, neither more nor less.

[12]Ibid., 34.

[13]Cornelius Krahn, *Menno Simons* (Karlsruhe: Heinrich Schneider, 1936), 105-107.

6 Mennonite Literary Voices: Past and Present

That plain, unrhetorical style, most likely coming directly from an oral tradition, is unmistakable in the doctrinal and pastoral writings of Menno, Dirk Phillips, and other Anabaptist leaders, although even they are often betrayed by their intense spiritual fervor into a more highly colored and tropistic rhetoric. When we turn to some of the most enduringly popular devotional books by Anabaptist writers, books like Peter Peters' *The Way to the City of Peace* and *The Mirror of Greed*, Schabalie's *The Wandering Soul*, the early martyr ballads in the Anabaptist hymnal *Ausbund*, and, above all, to van Braght's epic *Martyrs Mirror*, all of them designed to provide an authentic and practical religious ideology, we become aware of a curious paradox. Intended as pious aids to worship that would justify the ways of God to Anabaptists, to adapt Milton's famous phrase, in a direct, unequivocal manner, they invariably take on the shape of literary myth, that is, they tell stories that appeal to the imagination in a literary way even as they instruct in a religious way.

All are in some sense literary allegories that tell a literal story on the surface but also signify a deeper, divinely correlated order of agents, concepts, and events. Very much in the oral tradition they depict allegorical voices, invented characters, or actual people speaking in down-to-earth dialogue in a sincere, folksy, deliberately unliterary style in which the signified thing (*rerum*) is much more important than the signifier (*verbum*). Nevertheless, what we should note about this artless rhetoric is that it *is* a rhetoric, a style, in spite of its unrhetorical pretense, a style that bears a much richer freight of implied meaning on its relatively bare surface than was consciously intended. My point is that these common elements reveal the rudiments of a Mennonite literary imagination and technique almost in spite of themselves.

A closer look at these Anabaptist popular writings will confirm the general points I have been making. That *Martyrs Mirror* can be regarded as a work of literature seems to me indisputable, even if we agree that it is a much greater religious work than it is a literary one. However loosely organized in form and formulaic in treatment, this magnificent Christian saga owes at least some of its enduring appeal to its literary characteristics. We know that the narrative accounts of Anabaptist martyrs came directly out of the oral tradition as stories that had been retold countless times before van Braght edited them in written form.[14] In terms of literary allegory, they form a vast series of exempla designed to teach Christians how to live and die in the faith. As oral stories they had already received much of their literary shaping, tone, and texture beforehand—in a few cases stories had already been turned into full folk myths with imaginative touches of the poetic and the supernatural.[15] While the historian may deplore such stories as lacking historical validation, the literary critic sees them as examples of the literary imagination at work.[16] Structurally, the personal narratives, usually told in a reportorial, austerely realistic style, are juxtaposed with hundreds of emotionally charged personal letters, moving confessions, and gripping trial transcripts, all in contrasting narrative styles and voices. The spare, distanced third-person narratives, the fervent first-person letters and confessions, and the dramatic arguments at the trials all combine to make up the richly textured narratology of *Martyrs Mirror*.

The master organizing metaphor of the book is indicated by its original title—"The Bloody Theatre"—a performing stage upon which martyrdom was enacted by a cast of ordinary people who became extraordinary physical and spiritual heroes by virtue of their courage, unshakable faith, and almost super-human conviction. The often protracted ritual of martyrdom, from arrest through imprisonment and trial to public execution, was not only a physical but an allegorical reenactment of the innocent suffering and martyrdom of the central figure and symbol of the Bible. Indeed, there is an almost histrionic quality in the words and behavior of many of the martyrs, at least as recorded by van Braght. Just how apt the metaphor of stage drama is to these proceedings has been pointed out recently by John S. Oyer and

---

[14]See Alan F. Kreider, "'The Servant is not Greater Than His Master': The Anabaptists and the Suffering Church," *Mennonite Quarterly Review* 58 (January 1984): 11.

[15]See, for example, the story of Leonard Keyser, who predicted that both his body and the flower he plucked on the way to his execution would survive the flames intact. (Thieleman J. van Braght, *The Bloody Theater or Martyrs Mirror of the Defenseless Christians* (Scottdale: Herald Press, 1972), 420-421) Or that of Hans Blietel, who foretold that his execution would be accompanied by a sign in heaven, which turned out to be a "darkened sun full of spots" and "a beautiful dove [flitting] from the fire and [flying] over him to heaven." (*Martyrs Mirror*, 474) And Mary van Beckum, who predicted (correctly) that the stake at which she was to be burned would "grow green" (*Martyrs Mirror*, 500).

[16]See for example C. J. Dyck, "The Suffering Church in Anabaptism," *Mennonite Quarterly Review* 59 (January 1985): 9, for the historian's view.

8 Mennonite Literary Voices: Past and Present

Robert Kreider, who identify the town square as the "stage," the martyrs as the "cast," the trial proceedings and confessional statements as the "script," the jailers, executioners, etc. as the "stagehands," the instruments of torture and execution as the "props," and the crowds of onlookers as the "spectators" who came to see a good show.[17]

Revealing as it is, however, the theatre analogy should not make us lose sight of the fact that language—language stripped to its life-and-death essentials—forms the heart of *Martyrs Mirror*. This is a "speaking" book in that the martyrs' own inspired words much more than the obscene physical facts of martyrdom bring home to the reader the spiritual and visionary dimensions of the Anabaptists' living liturgy. Even Jan Luyken's engravings, graphic and unforgettable as they are, are overwhelmingly earthbound, depicting almost exclusively the hideous last moments leading up to execution or else the banal repetitions of arrest and torture. Only a few of them manage to capture the spiritual joy and soul ecstasy of the martyrs.[18]

Most Anabaptist believers were arrested and sentenced for what they said and wrote rather than for overt actions. Criminals are convicted for their deeds, heretics for what they have spoken or written. And language used *in extremis,* so to speak, typically becomes eloquent and evocative no matter how simple the words, pointing beyond itself to higher allegorical or symbolic meaning, moving powerfully with existentially felt incisiveness and weight. Here is a brief example of an oral exchange that rises to the heights of the literary sublime even though the words are transparently direct, even prosaic:

Ques. "Who baptized you?"
Ans. "It does not behoove me to tell."
Ques. "We shall make you tell."
Ans. "My flesh is before you; do with it as you please."[19]

---

[17]John S. Oyer and Robert S. Kreider, *Mirror of the Martyrs* (Intercourse: Good Books, 1990), 13.

[18]In the Sohm translation, which reproduces only 55 of the original 104 etchings, a good four-fifths of them depict scenes of physical threat and violence, while only three of them could be said to depict spiritual or inspirational moments. Van Braght himself died a good twenty years before Luyken's copper plates were added to the 1685 edition, and one wonders what he would have thought of their heavy emphasis on the physical aspects of martyrdom. Would he have regarded them as working against his intentions, at least in part?

[19]*Martyrs Mirror,* 525.

This charged terseness of speech, this laconic (almost iconic) evocation of meaning, this solemn economizing of verbal means is deeply imbedded in the Anabaptist-Mennonite character, and is reflected in the written tradition of the plain style.

In the twenty martyrs ballads first included in the 1583 edition of the hymnal *Ausbund*, the compressed ballad form serves as a dramatic vehicle for the graphic stories told in plain style. Victor G. Doerksen, who has examined the literary qualities of these eloquently realistic hymn-poems, draws attention to their "basic simplicity and straightforwardness."[20] "The life depicted in [them]," he writes, "is an either-or proposition; the perception of reality is a perception of a battle between the forces of good and evil."[21] Doerksen, drawing on Goethe, points out that the ballad form "combines inextricably epic, dramatic and lyric elements,"[22] and that this condensed but powerful literary form is responsible for much of the profound emotional effect of these ballads. While the modern sensibility may be offended by the grisly details of violence so matter-of-factly described in these poems, they are nevertheless suffused with the dignity and spiritual affirmation we associate with the highest literary tragedy. The death of Jörg Wagner is described as follows (I have tried to preserve the rugged diction and metre of the German version in my translation):

> They lashed him to a ladder raw,
> Stoked well the wood and straw,
> Price of laughter now rose higher.
> Jesus, Jesus, loud he called
> A fourth time from the fire. (hymn 11:26)

Understatement and stark dramatic contrast are constituent elements of the plain style here.

Three of the most popular Anabaptist devotional books were Johann Phillip Schabalie's *The Wandering Soul* (1635-38), and Peter Peters' *The Way to the City of Peace* (c.1625) and *The Mirror of Greed* (1638). All three are written in the then popular literary form of Christian allegory in dialogue, of which the most famous example is of course Bunyan's *Pilgrim's Progress* (1678).

---

[20]Victor G. Doerksen, "The Anabaptist Martyr Ballad," *Mennonite Quarterly Review* 51 (January 1977): 20.

[21]Ibid., 20-21.

[22]Ibid., 8.

Schabalie's *The Wandering Soul*, having gone through almost a hundred editions in Dutch, German, and English, is arguably the most widely read Mennonite book ever. Almost forgotten today, it was immensely popular with both Mennonite and non-Mennonite readers down to the end of the nineteenth century.[23] The book's popularity is not difficult to understand. By writing a "factual" paraphrase of the Bible, Schabalie thought he was producing an accurate history of the world, and he wrote with such a sure-handed common touch that the book retains its narrative charm to this day. His method was to interweave biblical stories with material from a wide assortment of ancient writers like Eusebius, Pliny, and Josephus, adding his own imaginative details wherever they were needed.

The dialogue form with its unpretentious speakers and homespun conversations also adds to the illusion that this is factual history, a literal account of what happened in the Bible. At widely separated historical intervals the Wandering Soul, the allegorical quester in search of Truth, interviews Adam, Noah, and Simon Cleophas, respectively, getting in simple language an account of what happened during their time. The accounts are filled with homely details and folksy illustrations designed to appeal to simple, literal-minded readers. Adam, for example, relates that as soon as he and Eve were expelled from Paradise they developed "headaches, toothaches and other ailments,"[24] and complains that his wife, so amiable before, "when she saw that she was now to be submissive to me, sometimes became a little impatient, so that at times the result was quarreling and strife."[25] It is the plain style at its most convincing, serving up as it does an artless narrative sincerely presented as documented history.

Peter Peters' *The Way to the City of Peace* and *The Mirror of Greed*[26] are more freely invented allegories, although written in a relaxed, gentle plain style similar to Schabalie's. The City of Peace represents a kind of religious Utopia whose values and perfections Jan, the spiritual teacher, extols to Peter, the pilgrim

[23]See *Mennonite Encyclopedia* 4: 438, and Robert Friedmann, *Mennonite Piety Through the Centuries* (Goshen: The Mennonite Historical Society, 1949), 113-115.

[24]Johann Phillip Schabalie, *Die Wandelnde Seele* (Scottdale: Mennonite Publishing House, 1919), 12.

[25]Ibid., 13.

[26]A new German edition of *Spiegel der Gierichkeit*, published by the Kleine Gemeinde in 1827 was the first book produced by the Mennonites in Russia. See Delbert Plett, *The Golden Years* (Steinbach: D. F. P. Publications, 1985), 320.

eager to be instructed. The two engage in an amiable, informal conversation that covers such Anabaptist-Mennonite issues as discipleship, materialism, baptism, non-violence, and shunning. While devoid of any dramatic tension, the dialogue seems to come straight out of the oral tradition and sounds as natural and credible as a serious conversation between old friends. *The Mirror of Greed* is a more spirited and even more realistic allegory in which Gerhard (the name stands for greed) brazenly expounds on his philosophy of materialism only to be upbraided and brought to his senses by Friedenrick (again the name is allegorical), the wise counsellor who gently but firmly leads Gerhard back to the hard but exhilarating path of the true Christian.

The authors of these early Anabaptist devotional works represented the progressive, educated wing of Dutch Mennonitism and their reasons for writing as they did were practical and didactic. In the first half of the seventeenth century the Mennonites, having survived the horrors of persecution, were in the process of becoming prosperous and acculturated and therefore in need of devotional writing that was admonitory as well as inspirational and edifying. They were helping to forge a religious ideology for rank-and-file believers, presenting the values and doctrines of a developing Anabaptist-Mennonite church institution in a popular style that was meant to convey the truth in a literal, unambiguous, and unliterary manner.

What the modern reader sees in these early works is a literary imagination groping its way, feebly at times, more vigorously at others, towards freer modes of imaginative expression. And the plain style can be seen as a literary style no matter how devoid of literary pretensions. It is a literary language straining to be creative—plastic and evocative—within very tight rhetorical and theological restraints. What is striking about this writing is that it is never imposed from above as a product of high culture—the culture of Cain's race or Caesar's world—but that it comes from below, from an oral tradition of humble people and to be read by such people: hence, the predilection for the Spirit in human history presented as realistic history or, conversely, spiritual history presented as the actual experience of Everyman. And so from the beginning the Mennonite literary imagination seems to have been drawn to a gritty realism serving didactic purposes, as opposed to high fantasy or the free literary imagination. Allegory was a convenient form in that it allowed the realistic surface of the writing to act as a springboard for a further moral or spiritual dimension of meaning. And that allegorical meaning could be more or less controlled and not allowed to spin off various unpredictable meanings as full-blown literary symbolism does.

The seventeenth-century Anabaptist written tradition was inherited by the Mennonites of the Vistula delta and in a modest way augmented by them. From there it was transported to Russia where it also helped to keep the literary imagination alive, even though Russian Mennonites, at least in the first half of the nineteenth century, were reduced to a mainly oral culture. Apart from the few inherited devotional books and the tract literature imported from Germany, there was not much by way of a print culture, and nothing at all by way of literary activity until the closing decades of the century.[27] By then there was a growing sense of ethnicity and cultural identity and an expanding, well-educated intellectual elite to give it voice in print, although the literary imagination was still dormant. Most of the writing in this period came from the pens of amateur historians and theologians.[28] The development of a literary imagination among Russian Mennonites was probably inhibited by the fact that while the educated elite wrote in High German, its language of high culture and literature, the daily experience of most Mennonites was encoded in *Plautdietsch*, which was not available as a written language and in any case was considered as nothing more than a peasant vernacular outside the sphere of high culture.

Nevertheless, *Plautdietsch* acted as a powerful ethnic shaping force in Russia, as it had done earlier in the Vistula delta. High German may have been the "official" language in which Russian

[27]A non-Mennonite writer who caught the imagination of many Mennonites in Russia in the nineteenth century was Johann Jung Stilling, a German Pietist writer whose allegorical novel *Das Heimweh* (1794) was regarded as an inspired prophecy for the end-times. Jung Stilling knew and valued the Mennonites and wrote about them in several of his books, including *Heimweh*. According to Victor Doerksen, Jung Stilling taught the Mennonite literary imagination how to "internalize" the spiritual quest by dramatizing it as a thrilling search for a true home, a mystic journey divorced from the harsh realities of the outer world. See Victor G. Doerksen, "From Jung Stilling to Rudy Wiebe," in *Mennonite Images: Historical, Cultural, and Literary Essays Dealing with Mennonite Issues*, ed. Harry Loewen (Winnipeg: Hyperion Press, 1980), and Doerksen, "In Search of a Mennonite Imagination," *Journal of Mennonite Studies* 2 (1984): 110-111. The theme of homesickness (*Heimweh*) reflects a restless spiritual yearning within "an artificial interior world" of the imagination which resulted in a "trivializing of religious experience," Doerksen argues, in stark contrast with the "tough realism and honesty" of Anabaptist writing (Ibid.).

[28]For a fuller account of these writers see my article "The Print Culture of the Russian Mennonites: 1870-1930" in *Mennonites in Russia: Essays in Honour of Gerhard Lohrenz*, ed. John Friesen (Winnipeg: CMBC Publications, 1989), 221-237.

Mennonites worshipped, read their Bible and traditional devotional books, carried on business correspondence, communicated with branches of the government, and read their own papers and German literature, but it was also a language growing ever more remote from its origins. High German constantly reminded them of their alienation from their past in Western Europe, specifically Germany, the country whose culture they claimed but with which they were physically and spiritually out of touch. *Plautdietsch*, however, was as warm and personal to the touch as their own bodies. In the absence of an indigenous literature, it provided an ongoing substitute in the form of oral story and folk legend, a kind of unwritten, subversive counter-literature consisting of never-ending streams of earthy, often humorous stories, everyday experiences fancifully embroidered, homely and pungent anecdotes, parodic wordplay, irreverent character sketches, and endlessly elaborated narratives passed on from generation to generation. The result was that most Mennonites in Russia lived a kind of linguistic double life: a sober, basically religious one in High German, and a more relaxed, more spontaneously creative one in Low German.

Plautdietsch may also have helped along a gradual drift towards secularization in Russian Mennonite society. Had there been a standard orthography for *Plautdietsch* it might even have developed a secular literature. James Urry has pointed out that when the earliest attempts at written *Plautdietsch* appeared in the secular, non-Mennonite paper *Odessaer Zeitung* in the early 1880s, they dealt not with religion or the church, but with such subjects as education and social mores.[29] A few years later, in 1886-87, there appeared in the same paper what was probably the first Mennonite fiction published in Russia. It consisted of a series of three short stories by Jacob Toews entitled "The Steppe in Winter," reminiscent in style and treatment of Turgenev's masterful *Sportsman's Sketches* (1852). The stories are realistically portrayed, and what is particularly interesting about the first two, which have Mennonite characters and settings, is that while the

---

[29]For specific references see *Odessaer Zeitung*, 273 (5/17 December 1882): 3; *Odessaer Zeitung*, 12 (16/28 January 1883): 1; and *Odessaer Zeitung*, 103 (6/18 May 1884): 2-3. See also Urry's insightful treatment of the influence of Low German on Mennonite identity in "From Speech to Literature: Low German and Mennonite Identity in Two Worlds," *History & Anthropology* 5 (1990): 91-116.

language of narration is High German, the dialogue of the Mennonite characters is entirely in *Plautdietsch*.[30]

By the centennial year of 1889 Russian Mennonite society was approaching full bloom economically and culturally (as always, the two were inextricably intertwined). Pride and confidence in its own achievements and ethnic autonomy had never been greater, although there would soon be disturbing signs of things to come.[31] The Russian Mennonites' triumphalist view of who they were and how far they had come as a people was further enhanced by their first attempts at historical self-definition. Written in High German by educated ministers and teachers, these early historical accounts and biographies, far from being works of objective scholarship, were really proto-literary works presenting the favorable historical and social myths by which the Mennonites of Russia wanted to be known and remembered.[32] Among the most important of these works were David H. Epp's pioneer history of the Old Colony, his biography of the influential leader Johann Cornies, and P.M. Friesen's massive *The Mennonite Brotherhood in Russia*, all of which served as fitting documentary legitimation just before the *Götterdämmerung* of the Mennonite commonwealth took place. They were ideological works, anecdotal and personal in tone, uncritical and almost narcissistically focussed on the Mennonite world.

The first expressly literary works by Mennonite authors also appeared in the years just before war and revolution struck. It was a very modest beginning consisting of a few volumes of verse, three Low German playlets, and three volumes of prose fiction, besides a scattering of verses, prose sketches, and short fiction in various periodicals and journals. The first Russian Mennonite to achieve recognition as a religious poet and hymn writer was the great revivalist minister Bernhard Harder (1832-1884), whose large output of devotional verse, hymns, and decorous occasional poems was published posthumously in 1888, the first such book to be published by Mennonites in Russia. Harder's religious poems are facile but sincere, technically adroit, and usually benign in tone. A few of his later occasional poems

---

[30]For a fuller account of these stories see my "The Print Culture of the Russian Mennonites: 1870-1930," 227.

[31]See James Urry, *None But Saints: The Transformation of Mennonite Life in Russia 1789-1889* (Winnipeg: Hyperion Press, 1989), 225ff. for a fine account of this phase of Russian Mennonite history.

[32]Again, I am indebted to Professor Urry for his written comments on this form of writing.

show signs of wanting to break out of the didactic mold, indicating that Harder might have been capable of becoming something more than a pulpit versifier. In 1895 Gerhard Loewen's *Feldblumen* appeared, a collection of lyric poems aesthetically inspired rather than relying on the clichés of religious verse. Loewen's delicate nature poems breathe of a natural reverence for God's created world, and while some are cast in a pale glow of pious sentimentalism, most are fairly fresh in form and treatment and secular in spirit, as Harry Loewen has shown.[33]

J.H. Janzen's ground-breaking 1910 collection of twelve didactic short stories—*For My Eyes Have Seen Thy Savior*—was well if somewhat cautiously received by Russian Mennonite readers, and by his own admission inspired the young Arnold Dyck to take Mennonite writing seriously.[34] Janzen also wrote three one-act plays in *Plautdietsch* which were performed by students in the school where he taught. *De Bildung* (*Education*) (1912), the first and best of them, was a comedy with a soft satiric edge on the timely issue of the cultural advantages of a secondary education. Not much regarded at the time, Janzen's plays were important in that for the first time ordinary Mennonite characters and their experiences were presented entirely in the language of those experiences. And they were deliberately written in a Low German plain style that pretended to be unliterary but was in fact highly evocative in literary meaning. The only other writer of fiction before the war was Peter B. Harder, the son of Bernhard Harder, who in 1913 published *Loose Leaves*, a volume of genre stories, as well as a novel—*Destinies: or the Lutheran Cousin*—a somewhat lurid domestic melodrama obviously designed to attract not only Mennonite readers in Russia but non-Mennonite readers in Germany. The volume of short stories contains some fine sketches based on Harder's own life and includes a good deal of dialogue in *Plautdietsch*.[35]

The tragic upheaval of war and revolution and the destruction of the Mennonite commonwealth in Russia shocked the Mennonite literary imagination into life as nothing had since the age of martyrdom. Not only was there a sense of faith, peoplehood, and identity in deadly peril, but suddenly there

---

[33]Harry Loewen, "Gerhard Loewen (1863-1946): Early Mennonite Poet, and Teacher," *Journal of Mennonite Studies* 9 (1991): 91-103.

[34]Arnold Dyck, "Jacob H. Janzen: Writer," *Mennonite Life* 6 (July 1951): 33.

[35]For a fuller account of these works see my article "The Russian-Mennonite Experience in Fiction," *Mennonite Images*, ed. Harry Loewen, 223-227.

were real-life villains (the terrorist leader Makhno and his kind) and heroes (the new Mennonite martyrs) in ready-made dramatic plots to write about. Swept away was the complacent old tradition of devotional and didactic writing, the sentimental accounts in the papers and journals of Mennonite bucolic bliss, of dreamy, self-absorbed village life. It was only in exile, however, that the reawakened literary imagination began to express itself in writing. In the 1920s and 1930s a small band of emigré writers, led by Arnold Dyck in Manitoba, produced a spate of semi-fictionalized memoirs and sketches, short stories, poems, and novels in which they tried to make sense of their traumatic suffering and loss. It was the beginning of Canadian Mennonite writing in German, the older *Kanadier* Mennonites not having up to that time produced a single literary writer of any merit.

Like emigré writers everywhere, the Russian Mennonites wrote about their lost homeland, the familiar world from which they had been exiled rather than the alien one in which they now found themselves. Canadian novelist Robert Kroetsch has noted that, "In ethnic writing there is often an attempt at healing by the rewriting of myths. The myth most often retold . . . is the garden story."[36] In their poems, stories, and novels these Mennonite writers idealized their ethnic Russian garden and evoked the tragedy of its desecration by the serpent of revolutionary violence. Among the prominent writers of that pioneer generation were J. H. Janzen, Gerhard G. Toews, Peter J. Klassen, Peter G. Epp and Dietrich Neufeld (the latter two in the U.S.), Fritz Senn (Gerhard Friesen), and, most important of all, Arnold Dyck.

What is new and different about these Mennonite writers is their thoroughly ethnic orientation and, for the most part, their secular stance. In the free environment of the Russian steppes, Mennonite society had achieved the most clearly defined ethnocultural identity in Mennonite history, and had managed to produce before its downfall the ·first and probably only generation of purely ethnocultural writers. While many Russian Mennonites experienced a spiritual reawakening as the result of their tragic suffering, their writers took a determinedly ethnic and secular direction. With the exception of J. H. Janzen, who became the bishop of his church in Ontario, none of the writers I have mentioned had close ties with the Mennonite church. Most

---

[36]Robert Kroetsch, "The Grammar of Silence: Narrative Patterns in Ethnic Writing," *Canadian Literature* 106 (1985): 69.

of them were relatively sophisticated men of the world who were Mennonites much more by virtue of birth, language, suffering, and loss than by religious conviction. Their lost Russian homeland was to them a physical place with an ethnic people, not the temporary home of pilgrims on the way to the heavenly kingdom. And their concept of ethnic identity was to a large extent modelled on the German concept of *Volk* and *Kultur*, and was tinged with the notion of racial purity and "Germanness" that prevailed in the Nazi Germany of the 1930s.[37]

As the leading light of this group, Arnold Dyck (1889-1970) had a keen perception of Mennonite ethnicity and the deep love and understanding of his people that enabled him to bring that perception to creative life. Dyck was an important literary figure who in spite of near-poverty and cultural isolation, not to mention culture shock and reader indifference, forged a distinguished career as a novelist, playwright, essayist, editor, publisher, and cultural entrepreneur from the 1920s through the 1950s. Trained as an artist and painter in Germany and Russia before World War I, he understood that *Plautdietsch* was the mother language of his Russian Mennonite *Völklein*, as he liked to call it, and so he wrote most of his best work in that picturesque language. Dyck showed that the plain style in Low German could yield delicious effects in the hands of a master ironist. His three comic novels about the travels of "Koop enn Bua," a pair of naive Manitoba farmers, as well as his short stories and plays in *Plautdietsch*, represent the finest achievement in Russian Mennonite writing.[38] And his sensitive recreation of the Russian Mennonite garden and the budding of his young protagonist's artistic consciousness within it in his *Bildungsroman, Verloren in der Steppe (Lost in the Steppe)*, captured the Mennonite experience in Russia in a definitive mythic form.

Without a doubt Arnold Dyck is our purest *ethnic* writer. Dyck saw his Mennonite world as a vital ethnic reality existing for its own cultural sake, not for the sake of the church as nurturing and controlling center. He secularized the teachings of the church into socio-ethnic values which give his peasant characters an appealing innocence and a fundamental dignity and decency never entirely lost even when skewed by oddities of behavior,

---

[37]One radical exception to this was Dietrich Neufeld, the author of *A Russian Dance of Death* and other books, who began as a socialist in Russia and later developed a rabid hatred of Nazi Germany.

[38]See my article "The Role of Arnold Dyck in Canadian Mennonite Writing," *Journal of Mennonite Studies* 9 (1991).

wilful blunders, and minor defects of character. In Dyck's essentially comic vision, evil exists only by implication, never by direct intervention. The dry, gentle irony that was his trademark seldom sharpened into satire and never degenerated into sentimentality. His driving motive as a didactic writer was to provide his people with a set of civilized cultural values.

Where Arnold Dyck went wrong was in assuming, along with other members of his writing generation, that the secularized ethnic and political vision brought from Russia could be transplanted to the New World intact, that it could resist the forces of assimilation and acculturation, to say nothing of a much more evangelical-minded body of believers in the Mennonite community here. By the 1940s, however, it was obvious even to Dyck that the kind of ethnic identity he approved was beginning to erode rapidly along with *Plautdietsch*, which was for him the *sine qua non* of that ethnic identity. His letters to friends and colleagues became increasingly bitter as he expressed his despair over the "Americanization" of his people, by which he meant a linguistic debasement from German to English which was leading to a general cultural vulgarization and a loss of civilized European values. In a late play never published or performed in his lifetime, one of his characters sums up Dyck's own forlorn position when he says, "homeless as we [Mennonites] are, [*Plautdietsch*] has itself been something like a homeland."[39]

Dyck refused to see that the transition from *Plautdietsch* and German to English did not automatically spell the end of Russian-Mennonite ethnic identity, that the essence of that experience and culture could be imaginatively preserved in English. And so, important as the writing in German of this emigré generation was, it dwindled into impotence and irrelevance because it refused to put down its roots in new cultural soil, failed to understand that English would for the first time provide Mennonite writers with a major literary language that would also be the language of their daily experience. Dyck and his literary colleagues had done much to prepare the Mennonite literary soil, but younger writers would soon take over and work it with new and more effective literary tools. That exciting new Mennonite literary scene in English is the subject of my second chapter.

---

[39] *Collected Works of Arnold Dyck*, eds. George K. Epp and Elisabeth Peters, vol. 4 (Winnipeg: Manitoba Mennonite Historical Society, 1990), 273.

Chapter 2

Where Was/Is the Place?

"One foot in, one foot out":
Themes and Issues in
Contemporary Mennonite Writing

As we have seen, from a modest, tentative beginning in Russia just before World War I, Mennonite literary writing in German was developed in Canada, and to a lesser extent in the U.S, by a generation of secularized emigré writers led by Arnold Dyck in the decades of the thirties through the fifties. Beginning in the 1960s with Rudy Wiebe and gaining momentum in the seventies and particularly in the 1980s, a new generation of Mennonite writers writing in English has been creating a body of literary works already far superior to that of its German-writing predecessors. Today's Mennonite writers are displaying technical skills, imaginative flair, and a boldness in addressing themselves to controversial issues and taboo themes never achieved by earlier Mennonite writers unassimilated to mainstream North American society. University educated and fully at home in a secular culture, contemporary Mennonite writers are no longer "in-house" artists satisfied with only Mennonite readers, but aspire to a more general readership.

Indeed, it is a startling paradox that most of our better writers today, particularly in Canada, are no longer Mennonites at all. That is, they are no longer Mennonites in the traditional sense of being Anabaptist-Mennonite Christians living as members in good standing of a Mennonite church within a well-defined ethnic community. Rather, they regard themselves simply as Canadian or American writers making literature out of whatever ethnic and religious experience they remember from their formative years. Where the German-writing generation of Arnold Dyck had a centripetal relationship with the Mennonite community, at least in an ethnic sense, the new generation of writers for the most part has an uneasy centrifugal relationship that in some cases threatens to fly apart completely. Having either left the Mennonite church or never joined it in the first place, these writers draw what creative energy they can from the tension generated between their remembered ethnic experience and their rejection of Mennonite faith and doctrine. By their own admission they are disenchanted with their Mennonite identity and heritage and write out of anger with whatever critical detachment they can muster. But not with indifference. Even the more dissident of them still seem to care deeply about their people even as they challenge Mennonite values. As one young Mennonite poet has expressed it: "i am in love not with what my people are but with what they want to be."[1]

One is tempted to say that Mennonite literature in English was invented by Rudy Wiebe in the early sixties, but of course that would be an oversimplification. In Canadian terms the claim might be valid, but in the U.S there was at least some Mennonite literature before that, although the output was sparse and generally mediocre in quality, as Elmer Suderman has shown.[2] Apart from Gordon Friesen's prairie-gothic novel *The Flamethrowers* (1936), Otto Schrag's *The Locusts* (1942), Helen Brenneman's *But Not Forsaken* (1955), Warren Kliewer's early short stories and plays, and Elmer Suderman's poems about Mennonite rural life, there is not much of any real merit before the sixties. In Canada, Mabel Dunham's pioneer novel *The Trail of the Conestoga* (1924) and Paul Hiebert's *Sarah Binks* (1947) were even more isolated literary phenomena and can in any case be regarded only peripherally as "Mennonite" works.

Today most of the best Mennonite writing is coming from Western Canada, most specifically Winnipeg and Manitoba, where a close-knit circle of Mennonite writers is at work shaping the Mennonite experience into literary art by creating a sense of imaginative place and situating in it literary myths that can help us to understand ourselves more clearly, inspiring us to take a closer look at ourselves and our Mennonite values, our aspirations and claims to being a community of faith and ethnic identity.

That this unprecedented concentration of Mennonite writing should be happening in this particular part of the scattered Mennonite world is not fortuitous, although to outsiders it may seem so. Some of the reasons are obvious. Western Canada, Manitoba in particular, has by far the largest number of Dutch-Russian Mennonites in North America, with anywhere between 20,000 and 40,000 in Winnipeg alone, depending on one's definition of "Mennonite." Secondly, we have seen that the Russian-Mennonite immigrants of the 1920s brought with them

---

[1]Audrey Poetker, *Prairie Fire* 11 (summer 1990): 119.

[2]Elmer Suderman, "Universal Values in Rudy Wiebe's *Peace Shall Destroy Many*," *Mennonite Life* 20 (October 1965): 172-173.

not only a well-defined ethnic culture but the rudiments of a literary tradition, albeit in German. They also became much more rapidly urbanized than the older Canadian-Mennonite groups.

Less obvious, perhaps, is the fact that the development of Mennonite ethnic culture in Western Canada and more recently the rise of Mennonite art and literature, coincided with the cultural development and the rise of the arts in Western Canada as a whole. Remote geographically from the rest of Canada and spiritually and culturally isolated from it in significant ways, the Canadian prairies, with their harsh climate and thin population, were forced to develop an indigenous culture or remain a wilderness, and the Dutch-Russian Mennonites came along at just the right time to help shape the culture and literature of this vast but solitary region.

Alienation, combined with a strong sense of difference from the rest of the world, the epic struggle to subdue the land, the protective shell of homogeneous communities—all of these conditions were of course familiar to Mennonites coming from the Russian steppes. Even so, in the classic pattern of immigration it took two to three generations for these Mennonites to feel enough like native Canadians to adopt Canadian culture while still retaining a semblance of Mennonite ethnic identity. As for literature, while the tradition of Canadian prairie realism in the novel goes back to the twenties and such writers as Frederick Phillip Grove, Robert Stead, and Laura Goodman Salverson, Western Canadian literature, indeed Canadian literature as a whole, did not gain real momentum until after World War II, at the very time when Mennonite cultural and linguistic assimilation was taking place.

And so Mennonite writers in the Canadian West have had the enormous advantage of helping to establish a Western Canadian literary identity merely by writing out of their own Mennonite experience and exploiting their sense of ethnic difference. Rudy Wiebe is not just an important Mennonite writer. As a literary heir of the prairie realists he has become one of the leading novelists in Canada. Compare that with the situation in the U.S, where Mennonite writers are for the most part anonymous voices lost on the vast stage of a much older, much larger, much more mature national literature. Canadian-Mennonite writers are helping to "name," in the biblical sense, to humanize and mythologize the Canadian West in a way that even a much larger group of American-Mennonite writers could never hope to do for the Midwest, say. Rudy Wiebe expressed his literary credo with exuberant confidence some twenty years ago:

[T]o break into the space of the reader's mind with the space of this western landscape and the people in it you must build a structure of fiction like an engineer builds a bridge or a skyscraper over and into space. A poem, a lyric, will not do. You must lay great black steel lines of fiction, break up that space with huge design and, like the fiction of the Russian steppes, build giant artifact.[3]

That brash confidence, the confidence of a talented literary mythmaker, has not only sustained Wiebe's own successful career as a novelist, but has served as a model for younger Mennonite writers.

Furthermore, the acculturation of Mennonites in Western Canada happened in little more than a generation, a much shorter time than it took in the U.S; it also happened much later and went hand-in-hand with the process of urbanization and the pursuit of higher education. All these social, cultural, and linguistic changes coming more or less at the same time have created an exciting sense of liberation among Canadian-Mennonite writers and artists, often resulting in yet another productive creative tension, the tension set up between memories of a rustic childhood and youth in a traditional Mennonite community, and the experience of a much more sophisticated urban adulthood. Hildi Froese Tiessen calls today's Mennonite writers "immigrants within the dominant Canadian culture," and makes the point that "Mennonite literature . . . in Canada today is unique because the very particular experiences about which these people write will not ever recur."[4] It is also true that almost all Canadian-Mennonite writers were nurtured on *Plautdietsch* as children, which means that vestiges of the Low German oral plain style are still to be found in their English wri ting.[5]

---

[3]Rudy Wiebe, "Passage by Land," in *Writers of the Prairies*, ed. Donald G. Stephens (Vancouver: University of British Columbia Press, 1973), 131.

[4]Hildi Froese Tiessen, "Mennonite/s Writing in Canada: An Introduction" to *The New Quarterly: Special Issue: Mennonite/s Writing in Canada* 10 (Spring/Summer 1990): 12.

[5]The coming of age of Canadian Mennonite writing was dramatically evident at a special conference on Mennonite literature held at Conrad Grebel College in May 1990, and sponsored by *New Quarterly Review*, a non-Mennonite academic journal at the University of Waterloo in Ontario. Not only Mennonite writers participated in this conference, but some of Canada's leading non-Mennonite writers as well. In addition to numerous individually published Mennonite literary works, three anthologies of Mennonite literature have been published in

It is precisely those creative tensions between place and culture and between literary and ethnic languages which give a writer a sense of "doubleness," of having "one foot in, one foot out," in Patrick Friesen's phrase, and provide him with a "motive for metaphor" through which, in all his writing, he tries to find his way home again, to write himself and his place into imaginative existence, to create the authentic world of the imagination in which he and we, as readers, can live. The Russian Mennonite emigré writers did that by nostalgically recreating their remembered Russian garden as a metaphor expressing their "longing for a lost homeland," to borrow Harry Loewen's phrase.[6] Our new Mennonite writers are busy creating a world of the imagination which challenges us to re-examine our remembered Mennonite garden, to explore critically our inherited beliefs and values, to lay aside our accumulated prejudices, our fears and anxieties, and accept a finer, broader, more tolerant vision of ourselves. Maurice Mierau, another of the younger Canadian-Mennonite poets and critics, describes the high calling of Mennonite writers with trenchant irony:

> But whether Mennonite writers work apart from or within the tradition, they seem to be attracted to the prophetic and didactic modes of the 'outsider'—the same modes in which our preachers and theologians have announced the all-importance of God's Word, and the spiritual irrelevance of art.[7]

No writer has exemplified the serious aims and the prophetic-visionary mode of Mennonite writing more completely than Rudy Wiebe, who almost singlehandedly started it all. From the beginning he has been the quintessential Mennonite writer who speaks from within the community but who adopts in his fiction the radical Christian stance of the outsider, that is, the responsible critic who refuses to replicate the comfortably

---

Canada in the past two years. Mennonite writers like Rudy Wiebe, Armin Wiebe, Di Brandt, and others are regularly invited to German, French, Canadian, and American universities to read from their works and as writers in residence and as instructors of creative writing. Theses on Mennonite writing are also beginning to appear in Europe as well as in North America.

[6]See Harry Loewen,"Canadian Mennonite Literature: Longing for a Lost Homeland," *The Old and the New World: Literary Perspectives of German-Speaking Canadians,* ed. Walter Riedel (Toronto: University of Toronto Press, 1984).

[7]Maurice Mierau, *Prairie Fire* 11 (summer 1990): 139.

idealized image the community wishes to perpetuate. Elmer Suderman's perspicacious comment in an early analysis of Wiebe's first novel could be applied to all of his Mennonite novels:

> [Wiebe's] novel is not a lyrical soporific to restore faith's flagging energies but a sacrament of disturbance involving the reader in the most drastic sort of exposure to unwelcome experience and unfamiliar truth.[8]

Note that inspired oxymoron "a sacrament of disturbance," which captures the very essence of what not only Rudy Wiebe but other serious Mennonite writers are attempting to do in their work.

Peace Shall Destroy Many, Rudy Wiebe's controversial first novel, was published in 1962, only two years after Arnold Dyck's last novel, thus maintaining at least a chronological continuity with the German tradition, if not much else. By bringing to bear, unlike most of his Russian-Mennonite predecessors, a deeply religious literary sensibility, Wiebe was able to get under the skin of Mennonite readers much more effectively than Dyck's generation of largely secularized writers had done. Judged as literature, *Peace Shall Destroy Many* is apprentice work of much less power than his later novels, but its didactic intensity and fearless handling of important themes were enough to set the teeth of conservative Mennonite readers—and non-readers—on edge. *Peace* was the right novel at the right time in that it raised crucial questions and long-suppressed issues of Mennonite life and faith and dared to address them honestly and with creative independence. It slaughtered the sacred cows of institutionalized Mennonitism on all sides by dramatizing such issues as Mennonite isolationism and the patriarchal tyranny it bred, racial bigotry as the ugly product of Mennonite pride, passive non-resistance in a time of national crisis, the German versus English language crisis, sexual repression and subjugation of the woman, religious formalism and the lust for land which in league with religious formalism becomes such a soul-numbing form of idolatry. Even less forgivable in the eyes of many Canadian Mennonites, through the tyrannical character of Deacon Block the novel had the audacity to show that these sacred cows had been imported from Russia, where they had been sheltered in the Mennonite garden all along, and that the fondly remembered

[8]Suderman, 175.

garden had been tainted by sin and violence from within long before it was destroyed from without.

And so Wiebe was hounded out of the Mennonite community in Winnipeg because Canadian Mennonites were not yet ready to accept the authentically imagined world and characters he had invented for them. But he had set the agenda, an agenda of themes and issues he would continue to explore in subsequent novels and which he made it respectable for younger Mennonite writers to develop as well. In his first two novels—*Peace Shall Destroy Many* and *The Blue Mountains of China* (1970)—Rudy Wiebe created a Mennonite literary world real enough and spacious enough to make it possible and indeed respectable for other writers to "write Mennonite" even if they were themselves no longer practising Mennonites. He gave them a literary context in which to express Mennonite experience never before accessible to the creative imagination.

Wiebe's novelistic art as it developed over two decades in his three Mennonite novels from *Peace* to *My Lovely Enemy* (1983)—there are also four critically acclaimed non-Mennonite novels in between—shows an enormous growth in technical skills, depth, and in the handling of themes and language. *Peace* was conventional enough in form and simple enough in style to encourage ordinary Mennonites to read it, even though many of them misread it completely as fiction, including some Mennonite reviewers who should have known better.[9] In subsequent novels Wiebe perfected forms and styles so complex as to make them comprehensible only to more sophisticated readers (which of course did not prevent some Mennonite readers from misreading them even more egregiously).

In *Peace* Wiebe had chosen for his setting the kind of remote, claustrophobic Mennonite community in which he himself had grown up in northern Saskatchewan. In *The Blue Mountains of China* he presented a sweeping panorama of Mennonite wandering and settlement on four continents over a span of several generations. Written as a series of loosely but subtly related and vividly conceived separate episodes or short stories, the novel is deliberately disjunctive in form and structure, its style ambiguously complex, its themes, characters, and action presented in an oblique and visionary manner. There is no coherently developed plot, no central protagonist, no one

---

[9]See for example the review by Marlin Jeschke in *Mennonite Quarterly Review* 37 (October 1963): 135-137.

definitive point of view, the main elements we expect in a literary epic. And that deliberately disjunctive form itself reflects Wiebe's view of the collective Russian Mennonite world as less purposeful, coherent, and homogenous than it traditionally assumed itself to be.

The novel deals powerfully with such contrasted themes as betrayal and sacrifice in Russia, community solidarity and sexual repression in Paraguay, crass materialism and radical Christian discipleship in Canada. Of special interest here is Wiebe's subtle and eloquent use of oral voice and various levels of language of which the common denominator, the one remaining thread of continuity, is *Plautdietsch*. This is especially evident in the concluding scene where characters from diverse social, cultural, and linguistic backgrounds come together by carefully contrived chance to discuss *opp Plautdietsch* what it means to be Mennonite. In the end, however, nothing is resolved, all possibilities are left open and fluid as indicated by the chapter heading "On the Way." Even the radical Christian rhetoric of young John Reimer, dragging his symbolic cross along the highway, is subtly undercut by the dogged literalism and skeptical stoicism of the old Russian camp survivor Jakob Friesen.[10]

My Lovely Enemy, Wiebe's most recent Mennonite novel, is a profoundly Christian work of almost unbearable intensity, an extended parable about love and language which employs post-modern and magic realism techniques and a style so charged metaphorically that the novel reads like a prose poem in places. The novel takes us to the very edge of the mystery of life and death where even language cannot leap across the void to where the voiceless spirit lives in the "peace that passes understanding." Even more than *Blue Mountains*, this is a complex and layered didactic novel that spurns egotistical preaching, avoids the shelter of doctrine, rejects the claims of moral rectitude, and refuses to provide a logical, coherent pattern of thematic closure in its conclusion.

In *My Lovely Enemy* history professor James Dyck, a lapsed Mennonite, goes on a spiritual quest during which he explores love in all its forms and guises, from the frankly sexual to the

---

[10]See Ina Ferris, "Religious Vision and Fictional Form: Rudy Wiebe's *The Blue Mountains of China*," 95-96, and Magdalene Falk Redekop, "Translated Into the Past: Language in *The Blue Mountains of China*," 119-121, both articles in *A Voice In The Land; Essays By and About Rudy Wiebe*, ed. W. J. Keith (Edmonton: NeWest Press, 1981), for two different but interesting analyses of the concluding scene in the novel.

purest spiritual love with various gradations in between, including his adulterous love for a colleague's young wife, his deep love for his own wife and young daughter, and his special love for his aging mother. Through scenes of physical intimacy and discussions on the complex nature of love, including two astonishingly suggestive "interviews" with Jesus himself, Dyck begins to learn that love is one and indivisible and that the various categories into which we normally divide love—spiritual love, maternal love, parental love, romantic love, adulterous love—are artificially forced upon us by language and social codes. The theme of love triumphant as one indivisible whole transcending all logic and analysis, a truth beyond even metaphysical expression, receives its most dramatic treatment in the concluding scene where at the funeral of Dyck's mother she is miraculously restored to life and joins her son, the two women and daughter he loves, and the others at the funeral in a sacrament of potato salad and cold tea in the harvest field beside the cemetery. It is a love feast that goes beyond language and understanding, on a literal level resolving nothing (James Dyck is still an adulterer who wants to have his cake and eat it too), on a spiritual level resolving everything in a context that makes the literal irrelevant.

The central theme of interaction among community, family and individual explored by Rudy Wiebe in his three Mennonite novels is also prominent in the work of other Mennonite writers. A brief discussion and comparison of four works which portray life in fictitious Mennonite rural communities in southern Manitoba at different periods ranging from around World War I through the 1980s will serve as illustrations. Taken together these works give us a more or less consecutive account of the pressures and processes of change that Canadian Mennonite society has been subjected to in the past several generations. The main focus in all four works is the struggle for individual identity and meaning within a church-dominated, conformist society whose highest priority is to preserve itself.

Patrick Friesen's narrative poem *The Shunning* (1980) takes place early in this century in a tiny farming community that isn't even given a name. The story unfolds mainly on the two farms of the brothers Peter and Johann Neufeld, but offstage lurks a repressive little society dominated by an all-powerful, legalistic church run by petty, vindictive men. Symbolically, Peter's farm is a garden, but with a snake in it poised to strike. Peter himself is an innocent idealist, a fool of Christ—his brother Johann calls him *"der blaue Engel"*—who yearns for the purity and simplicity of the Christian love we associate with the Anabaptist ideal and who tries to ignore the church as an institution. For his "sin of pride" he is banned by Loewen, the church elder, shunned by his own wife, and driven to suicide because he literally "had nowhere to go."[11]

The second half of the poem is devoted to Johann, who loved his defiant brother Peter but who is willing to make the necessary compromises that enable him to survive in this cruel, claustrophobic religious atmosphere. Unlike his ascetic brother, Johann is a caring, sociable man who reaches out to others and lives a relatively rewarding life within the narrow constraints of a community in which an appreciation of beauty, sensuality, and joy are only clandestinely possible, if at all. The two brothers can be seen as representing two different sides of the Mennonite psyche—Peter the idealist pure of heart and soul but unwilling to compromise with reality, Johann the pragmatist to whom "time happens," willing to surrender his innocence as the price of survival in a closed church society oblivious to the outside world.

An American Mennonite, Warren Kliewer, nevertheless set his collection of related short stories *The Violators* (1964) in Waldheim, again a fictional village in southern Manitoba. His village characters are identified only as "German," though internal evidence in the stories leaves no doubt that they are Mennonite. Kliewer was apparently trying to avoid having his fictional world confused with his home town of Mountain Lake, Minnesota, a prudent subterfuge given the fierce territorial instincts of rural Mennonites.[12] Waldheim, as the name indicates, is both physically and spiritually isolated from the outside world, and the stunted parochialism of its inhabitants is rendered with almost grotesque realism in some of the ten stories in the book. The stories embrace the middle decades of the century, a time when the traditional remoteness from the world was about to be breached by linguistic change from German to English, by radio and TV, and other irresistible forces of assimilation.

---

[11]Patrick Friesen, *The Shunning* (Winnipeg: Turnstone Press, 1980), 43. This narrative poem was turned into a stage play by Friesen and performed to considerable popular and critical acclaim from October 10 to November 3, 1985, at Prairie Theatre Exchange in Winnipeg.

[12]In his introduction to the volume, Elmer Suderman wisely cautions the reader not to be deflected from the universality of Kliewer's stories by trying "to find a prototype for his community and for the German church" (xiii).

The stories deal with such themes and issues as spiritual pride, moral smugness, superstition, hypocrisy, sexual repression, lack of charity, and racism (against the local French Canadians). Reverend Schultz, the local pastor, is a pious, cliché-babbling inanity who symbolizes the spiritual sterility of the church, while other characters bring out the narrow, backward cultural state of the community. Stories like "The Death of the Patriarch" and "Martin and the French" vividly illustrate that Waldheim, far from being an idyllic spiritual retreat and refuge from the wicked city, harbors the destructive human ego with its cruelty and violence as much as any city. And yet, a few of these stories, most notably "UHF," one of the best in the book, also hint at a possible accommodation with the outside world, an end to benighted spiritual isolation and social alienation of the kind from which there seemed to be no escape in *The Shunning*.

Armin Wiebe's *The Salvation of Yasch Siemens* (1984) is a comic novel with serious undertones set in Gutenthal, another fictional Mennonite community in southern Manitoba as it was in the late fifties through the seventies. While still church-oriented, Gutenthal is in the throes of changing from a sleepy Mennonite farming community to a more progressive community culturally and technologically connected to the rest of the world. In the comic vision of the novel, the church is neither a repressive nor a dominant force, but is depicted as an institution comfortably integrated with an ethnic community confident of its own identity while casually adopting secular ways and customs from the outside world. The novel reflects the rapid secularization of Canadian society after the 1950s, with the church forced to adapt itself to the changed social conditions. At their best, church and ethnic community achieve an almost ideal balance or integration, as in an early scene where the traditional Sylvester (New Year's) Eve service is noisily interrupted by a gang of schoolboys dressed as mummers celebrating with the traditional *brummtopp*, a crude, home-made drum producing loud, flatulent sounds when worked with a horse tail. The raucous scene ends harmoniously, however, with the congregation lustily singing the Beethoven-Schiller Ode to Joy to the hoarse accompaniment of the lowly *brummtopp*.

Yasch Siemens, the comic hero, landless and fatherless (his father had defected to Mexico years earlier) and without status in the community, is forced to pull himself up by his own bootstraps, to gain local respectability by acquiring his own land along with a wife and family and membership in the church. With something of the picaresque hero in his makeup, Yasch, after numerous false starts and misadventures, finally acquires land and wife in one fell swoop by marrying the enormously fat but amiable Oata Needarp, who has just inherited her father's farm. In conjunction with Yasch's own shrewd mother, Oata teaches him the practical ways of the world and explodes the fallacy of his romantic fantasies. And so Yasch's "salvation" is much more a matter of gaining status in the ethnic community and life as a conservative farmer and landowner than salvation in the religious sense. As a somewhat aimless and self-destructive individualist, Yasch has to learn how to "connect" with the community and with the other individuals in his life, how, in short, to become a useful member of Mennonite society and a caring human being.

The language of *The Salvation of Yasch Siemens* deserves special mention. A unique form of English vernacular larded with Low German words and idioms literally translated ("overset"), it is the perfect vehicle not only for the comedy in the novel, but even more importantly for the presentation of an ethnic society in which the everyday Low German vernacular provided a lusty, irreverent counter-language to the solemn spiritual language of the church. Armin Wiebe cleverly exploits the Mennonite plain style derived from that oral tradition—he always refers to it as "Flat German," a literal translation of *Plautdietsch*—and forges it into a wonderful style whose hybrid strength and raw energy are fully up to his comic demands. Here, for example, are Yasch's reflections after fat Oata's father dies and Yasch realizes that his casual involvement with her now calls for a more serious commitment:

> A man can't just claw out from a woman like that, at least not if she has just found out that her Futtachi has gone dead. I mean if a person goes dead you can't just turn away and spin your tires. Not if you want to call yourself a mensch. A mensch has to deal with other mensch and when you try to do something with another mensch it always gets kompliziet. And when you try to do something with a fruemensch it can be like building a fence with hackelwire you found at the mist acre. But that's the ball game.[13]

[13]Armin Wiebe, *The Salvation of Yasch Siemens* (Winnipeg: Turnstone Press, 1984), 75.

Douglas Reimer's first collection of short stories, *Older Than Ravens* (1989), portrays life in the Manitoba community of Altwelt from the 1960s through the eighties. The very name of the village—Old World—implies that the place is an anachronism for the most recent generation of Mennonites growing up in it. In these intensely personal stories the solidarity of the traditional Mennonite community is breaking down, its rigid codes of belief and behavior expressed as mindless piety and insensitive social reflexes. Most of the stories are about three adolescent brothers, Peter, Thomas, and Roley Regier, who try to find themselves as individuals within a family and community where traditional Mennonite values and beliefs are being trivialized by the new "conversion" mentality represented by the Brunk Tent Mission. As a consequence, the brothers suffer from crippling feelings of guilt and religious *angst*, not to mention moral confusion, as they rebel against the narrow code of belief imposed upon them.

Well schooled in post-modernism, Douglas Reimer deals tellingly with such taboo subjects as adolescent sexual obsessions, sexual repression in parents, the hypocrisy of professing Christians, the spiritual shallowness of the "are you saved?" approach, and the suppressed violence that seems to lurk at the heart of Mennonite meekness and humility. "A Picture of Jesus" is the disturbing story of Thomas Regier, who in self-righteous imitation of Christ has the school principal spank him for a misdemeanor he knows other boys committed. By the time he gets home, however, he is close to hysteria and makes his mother put away her kitchen knife for fear that he may erupt in an act of violence—against himself possibly, or even against his mother.

The disturbing paradox of Altwelt is that while it considers itself an exemplary Christian community with all the answers, it actually provides no coherent pattern by which to live in today's world. A perceptive reviewer of Reimer's book states:

> In all honesty it must be said that the religion depicted in these stories is for the most part profoundly pathological. While these Mennonites are deeply burdened for the salvation of what they understand to be "the world," it was their own religion which stood most in need of redemption.[14]

---

[14]Denis R. Janz, review in *Mennonite Reporter* 20 (February 5, 1990): 9.

For all that, Reimer's troubled adolescent characters grow up into upwardly mobile middle-class Mennonites, enlightened enough to escape to the more tolerant world of the city, or else defiantly trying to enlarge their horizons in Altwelt. Either way they will never completely free themselves of the pervasive sin and guilt they experienced in the agonizing process of growing up in that community.

So far we have looked at the sense of place in Mennonite literature mainly in terms of how the individual relates to church and community. Mennonite writers also have a lot to say about relationships within the family. The traditional structure of the Mennonite church and community took the form of a patriarchal hierarchy with God the Father and Christ the Bridegroom as models for the church fathers (the minister-teachers) and for the father as head of the family. Not surprisingly the authoritative father, either as direct or implied metaphor, appears frequently in Mennonite literature. The traditional image is that of the benign, all-protective, life-giving, life-sustaining, wise, and justice-dispensing paterfamilias whose will and word must not be questioned, and who is himself answerable only to the church fathers and ultimately to God. He is the bearer of ancestral traditions, the connecting link, along with the grandfather, between the generations, the perpetuator of community wisdom and spokesman for those who depend upon him. In his purest form, he is a farmer, a tiller of the soil like Adam the first father, strong, stern, sparing of words, but resonating mysterious, even feared depths hidden from his subjects, that is, his wife and children. He is held in awe and veneration by his family, but, like God his model, he tends to be remote, not easily approachable.[15]

This god-like father appears frequently in the earlier Mennonite literature in German, where his strength and wisdom are freely acknowledged but his weaknesses and vulnerabilities seldom touched upon, at least not until he dwindles into feeble and passive grandfatherhood. But he is given some human touches. The traditional father in Arnold Dyck's *Lost in the Steppe*, for example, becomes addicted in middle age to the reading of

---

[15]I am indebted in a general way for insights into the Mennonite father image to Victor G. Doerksen's suggestive paper "'Our Father, Which Art in Heaven . . .': Some Thoughts on the Father Image in Recent Mennonite Poetry," in *Acts of Concealment: Mennonite/s Writing in Canada*, ed. Hildi Froese Tiessen and Peter Hinchcliffe (Waterloo, Ontario: University of Waterloo Press, 1992), pp. 39-51.

novels serialized in the German papers he takes in.[16] Fritz
Senn's many father poems, while portraying the hard-working
farmer-father, also show him coming home from the field out of
sorts and scolding the children, or coming out of his habitual
silence with friendly advice to his son, or relaxing in the evening
with his family around him.[17] By and large, however, in the
older Mennonite literature the father is presented in terms of the
traditional stereotype.

In Mennonite literature in English, the patriarchal image of the
father is no longer idealized but more ambiguously presented, as
in the character of Deacon Block in *Peace Shall Destroy Many*. As
the patriarchal leader of the isolated community he has
established in the Saskatchewan bush, Block is generous and
benign in helping those in need, but a tyrant in his attempts to
keep his community "pure" and uncontaminated by "the world."
Worse still, as family father, like Milton's Satan he tries to make
evil his good as he ruins his daughter's life with his cruel
repression, finally destroying her altogether. Earlier in Russia, he
had even committed murder in order to save his starving infant
son's life out of ego-driven dynastic motives.

The father-son relationship is a frequent theme in Mennonite
literature written by men and can take various ambivalent forms.
Elmer Suderman's recent cycle of father poems, "A Mennonite
Father: New Poems,"[18] portrays the traditional father, now long
dead, through the elegiac memory of a son with subtly
ambivalent feelings towards his strong, God-fearing sire who
worked the land without benefit of modern technology, who was
untouched by culture and art, and who would probably, if he
were still alive, be spiritually concerned for his Ph.D.-bearing
son.[19] Even as the son celebrates the memory of his father, he
implicitly measures himself against him, wondering whether he
is worthy, trying to find words to fill in the father's past silence,
conscious of his responsibility for re-imagining the father back
into life.

> I think about him often, wondering
> about the stories he did not tell

---

[16]See Arnold Dyck, *Lost in the Steppe*, trans. Henry D. Dyck (Steinbach:
Derksen Printers, 1974), 159.
[17]See Fritz Senn, *Gesammelte Gedichte und Prosa*, ed. Victor G. Doerksen
(Winnipeg: CMBC Publications, 1987), 42-44, 61 et passim.
[18]In *Journal of Mennonite Studies* 7 (1989): 96-102.
[19]Ibid., 97.

> so I might tell for him
> stories that might be true.[20]

Thus the traditional father figure is subtly undercut by his incompleteness, his "lostness," by the necessity of the son to "complete" the father, to give him the "voice" in the present that he never had even in the past.

Complex and even more ambivalent father images inform some of the best work of David Waltner-Toews and Patrick Friesen, the two senior Canadian-Mennonite poets who between them have published nine volumes of verse since the mid-seventies. Like Rudy Wiebe, Waltner-Toews accepts his Mennonite heritage although that has not prevented him from being sharply critical of its excesses, pretensions, and other weaknesses. He grew up with the burden of having a father who was a prominent minister, college teacher, and church historian in the Canadian Mennonite community. As a result, by the poet's own admission, his father "never entered my poems until he died." The poems expressing his sense of loss are among Waltner-Toews's most moving, but like all good elegies they are also universalized and made the occasion for meditation. For him the Mennonite father as public icon must finally be humanized and domesticated in memory before he can be accepted as personal father image. In "Christmas, 1979," Waltner-Toews imagines his father coming back for a visit a year after his death and completing the family Christmas scene in a way that leaves the poet-son feeling consoled and at peace:

> I come from the kitchen
> a piece of cold turkey
> in my hand.
> My father looks comfortable
> as if he intends to stay
> a long time.[21]

Patrick Friesen's group of "pa" poems forms the core of his poetic exploration of the father image. What is only delicately hinted at in Elmer Suderman's father poems, namely the necessity for the son to redeem his father's lost presence, of

---

[20]Ibid., 102.
[21]David Waltner-Toews, *Goodhousekeeping* (Winnipeg: Turnstone Press, 1983), 61.

keeping faith with his father's past, with perhaps regret for
having lost the purity and simplicity of the old Mennonite
tradition, comes to the fore in various ambivalent ways in
Friesen's father poems. Friesen was a rebellious son and his
remembered father image is far from traditional: "pa" was as
vulnerable as he was strong; in contrast to Waltner-Toews's
public father, he was a very private man, not so much silent as
inarticulate in the face of things he didn't understand about life.
But he lived entirely for his family, a fact the rebellious son did
not come to appreciate until after his father's premature death
when there was no longer a need to voice grievances. In "pa
poem 4: naked and nailed," the poet depicts his father as a kind
of Christ figure crucified for love but unable to voice love, and
so the son is finally forced to express his own reluctant love:

> And see you old dead man
> how I start with my grievance
> and always end up with this Goddamned love
> but I tell you that won't happen every time
> or it'll kill me.[22]

Wayne Tefs, Friesen's friend and fellow-writer in Winnipeg,
has pointed out that the death of the poet's father coincided with
Friesen's "assumption of the role of poet,"[23] and that his "elegiac
effusions on the death of the familial father act as agents of
expiation" for his own loss of faith and his feeling of having
"betrayed his past and his culture, the history of his father and
his father before him."[24] But by exploring his own guilt and
voicing his concern over his betrayal, the poet begins to define a
new feeling of faith and qualified belief in his past, thus shifting
the blame from his father to himself, so to speak, as he expresses
it in "fatherless again":

> 1.
> rest old man I must love you
> I'm the boy who blames himself
> our people taught us and taught us didn't they?
> the ritual of betrayal and penance

---

[22]Patrick Friesen, *Unearthly Horses* (Winnipeg: Turnstone Press, 1984), 19.
[23]Wayne Tefs, "13 Ways of Looking at Pat Friesen," in *Contemporary Manitoba Writers*, ed. Kenneth James Hughes (Winnipeg: Turnstone Press, 1990), 58.
[24]Ibid., 60.

> I'm sorry I'm sorry I'm sorry
> if there is anything I can hate it's me[25]

The acceptance here is, of course, hesitant, provisional, and finally still ambivalent, but in the clash of dissonant notes the alert ear may also hear a chord of resolution.

I have been exploring in this chapter some of the central themes and issues that today's Mennonite male writers are addressing. In my next chapter I look at the ways in which Mennonite women writers are coming to grips—mainly in a feminist context—with the traditional image of the Mennonite woman as publicly invisible and voiceless. These women's voices, vibrant and controversial, are creating literary sounds never heard before in Mennonite writing.

[25] *Unearthly Horses*, 29.

Chapter 3

Where Was/Is the Woman's Voice?

The Re–Membering of the Mennonite Woman: Women Writing Within the Mennonite Ethos

In recent years the Mennonite literary scene has been dramatically enhanced by a growing group of talented women writers. Canadian Mennonite writers like Sandra Birdsell, Di Brandt, and Lois Braun already have international reputations, and poets like Sarah Klassen and Audrey Poetker, as well as Jean Janzen in the U.S., are also gaining the wider readerships they deserve. Indeed, without these powerful women's voices the Mennonite literary phenomenon of recent years could not have happened. Not only are these gifted women writing poems and short stories and novels which embody, like all good literature, our most vital experiences and visions, but perhaps even more importantly they are providing an eloquent collective voice for the Mennonite woman traditionally voiceless in public and visible only in private. As Hildi Froese Tiessen has pointed out, the voices of Mennonite women writers are "often projections of the authors' foremothers who suffered an enforced silence throughout the official histories of their people."[1]

Mennonite women historians and critics like Mary Lou Cummings, Katie Funk Wiebe, and Elaine Sommers Rich in the U.S. and Marlene Epp, Magdalene Redekop, and Carol Penner in Canada have begun to explore and redress the neglected story of women in Mennonite history and culture.[2] While valuable and authentic, these historical accounts and critical evaluations tend to be generalized, statisticized, and so cautiously documented that they seem somewhat muted and dry, lacking as they do the passion and drama of vividly realized literary voices. To my mind the most radical and persuasive "re-membering" of the Mennonite woman is being done through the literary imagination. That is where the compelling new voice of the Mennonite woman is coming from.

When, if ever in the past, did the Mennonite woman have a public voice and presence? Apparently she did, in the beginning.

---

[1] Hildi Froese Tiessen, Introduction to *The New Quarterly* Special Edition, 12.

[2] See, for example, Carol Penner, "Mennonite Women's History: A Survey," *Journal of Mennonite Studies* 9(1991): 122-135 for summaries of these and other women's writing on Mennonite women.

Before the Mennonite church became fully institutionalized, Anabaptist women had a strong voice and a very visible presence on the bloody stage of martyrdom. Almost a third of the approximately 1,000 martyrs identified by gender in *Martyrs Mirror* were women, and most of them underwent torture and execution as bravely as did the men. And even those numbers may not reflect accurately the importance of the public role women played within the Anabaptist movement.[3] While there is no conclusive evidence in *Martyrs Mirror* that any women were part of the formal church leadership (such as preachers and deacons), there is circumstantial evidence that a few, like Elisabeth Dirks and Aeffgen Lystyncx, were church teachers, while a few others like Goetken Gerrits and Vrou Gerrets are known to have written and published hymns.[4] Moreover, the many letters in *Martyrs Mirror* written from prison prove conclusively that Anabaptist women were well schooled in doctrine and in the Bible and eloquent in expressing their fervent faith.

Unfortunately, whatever equality of faith and martyrdom existed between Anabaptist men and women did not carry over into the spheres of marriage, church, and community.[5] Once the period of persecution was over and Anabaptist beliefs were codified and institutionalized, the public presence of women was over and they disappeared into their traditional roles as wives and mothers. Marlene Epp has argued that the "underside" of Mennonite history, i.e., the woman's side, reveals that Mennonite women have managed to acquire a public voice and presence in times of flux and crisis, "but [tend] to regress somewhat during times of community stability and status quo."[6] A modern example of this would be the courageous initiative with which Mennonite women in the Soviet Union organized clandestine churches in their homes while their men were still missing in the Gulag after World War II. However, when the men returned from exile they quickly took over these primitive but vital church

---

[3]According to *Mennonite Encyclopedia* 4: 973, women were often given milder sentences than death, which may in part account for the difference in number between male and female martyrs.

[4]See *Mennonite Encyclopedia* 4: 973.

[5]See M. Lucille Marr, "Anabaptist Women of the North: Peers in the Faith, Subordinates in Marriage," *Mennonite Quarterly Review* 61 (October 1987): 352 and passim.

[6]Marlene Epp, "Women in Canadian Mennonite History: 'Uncovering the Underside'," *Journal of Mennonite Studies* 5 (1987): 104.

cells and once again relegated their women to subordinate roles. We note also that in the aftermath of the Russian Revolution the official histories, public memoirs, and autobiographical novels were written by Mennonite men, but that some of the most dramatic and moving personal stories were written by women who had kept diaries and had an instinct for story-telling. Among the best of these are Maria Winter-Loewen's three-volume autobiography *Hoehen und Tiefen* (Peaks and Valleys), Susanna Toews' *Trek to Freedom*, Anna Reimer Dyck's *From the Caucasus to Canada*, Anita Priess' *Exiled to Siberia*, and *The Diary of Anna Baerg*. These stories were written by intrepid women who often had to follow their hazardous destinies alone, without the help of men, and became the stronger for it.

In a patriarchal society Mennonite women were expected to confine their activities to the traditional spheres of *Kirche, Kinder, und Küche* (church, children, and kitchen) and to fulfill themselves as best they could within the domestic sphere. They were voiceless and invisible in public and isolated from the rest of the world. In Russia very few Mennonite women spoke Russian, and even in Canada few rural women learned English before World War II. Such women were usually blissfully ignorant of the outside world and its culture. And yet the real story tellers in Mennonite families were often the mothers, secret readers who nurtured the creative spirit in their children and were frequently the custodians of the oral tradition within the family no matter how voiceless they were outside of it.

In my second chapter we saw how male Mennonite writers have dealt with the difficulties and complexities of the father-son relationship in a patriarchal society. The rebellious son is typically unable to come to terms with the all-powerful father figure until the father grows old or dies. Since the patriarch/father image represents not only social structures but the very ideology of the church, the son's rebellion is accompanied by feelings of guilt, a sense of betraying his Mennonite heritage. From a woman's perspective the picture is rather different. For one thing the guilt is missing. Instead there is a strong sense of victimhood as expressed by Mennonite women writers. Magdalene Redekop, in a passionate and brilliantly perceptive meditation on her own parents—her church leader father and sensitive, self-sacrificing mother—argues persuasively that the worst sin of a patriarchal society may be that it inspires a form of idolatry whereby the woman is allowed to love her Mennonite husband/father/patriarch only by sacrificing her own identity to him, by becoming his slave and making herself voiceless and invisible in subordination to him.[7] And Redekop pushes her argument to a radical feminist conclusion. "Oddly enough," she writes, "a Mennonite woman may have to become a feminist in order to become a Mennonite, if by this one assumes a radical Protestant stance that opposes idolatry and affirms the free choice of the individual.' [8]

As long as Mennonite literature was written mainly by men, the identity and role of the Mennonite woman was not explored in any great depth and of course from a predominantly male point of view. In her article "The Mennonite Woman in Mennonite Fiction," Katie Funk Wiebe tries to answer the question " Whois a Mennonite Woman?" by examining female characters in works of Mennonite fiction. Wiebe finds in them the female archetype of the Great Earth Mother split into the stereotypical female characters of "Eve Before the Fall" and "Eve After the Fall.' 'Eve Before the Fall is "a pure and asexual preserver of Mennonite faith and culture"[9] and can take various specific forms such as "the virtuous girl, the pious mother, or the saintly grandmother."[10] None of these types, of course, ever threatens the domination of the Mennonite man. Eve After the Fall represents the dark side of the Great Earth Mother, "the Mennonite woman's lower nature . . . controlled solely by womb and hands, not head and heart."[11] Less common in Mennonite fiction, according to Wiebe, is a "New Eve" who "rejects her restricted role in the Mennonite community and searches for ways to leave it if she cannot find a place in it, for to stay seems to her to require she become something other than what she is."[12]

It is precisely this rebellious New Eve who is the focus in much of the recent writing by Mennonite women. Unfortunately, Katie Funk Wiebe's article was written before most of the new women writers appeared on the scene with their militant New Eve characters and speakers. And even in the works she does examine she makes no conscious distinction between those

---

[7]Magdalene Redekop, "Through the Mennonite Looking Glass," in *Why I Am A Mennonite*, ed. Harry Loewen (Scottdale: Herald Press, 1988), 243 and passim.
[8]Ibid., 243.
[9]Katie Funk Wiebe, "The Mennonite Woman in Mennonite Fiction," in *Visions and Realities: Essays, Poems and Fiction Dealing with Mennonite Issues*, eds. Harry Loewen and Al Reimer (Winnipeg: Hyperion Press, 1985), 231.
[10]Ibid.
[11]Ibid., 241.
[12]Ibid., 232.

written by male authors and those written by women. And yet the three novels by Mennonite women writers which she discusses all make at least attempts to portray their female protagonists as New Eves, that is, as unwilling to conform to the traditional stereotypes of women. And if they fail to do this convincingly it is because all three portray rather weak or technically flawed female characters and not because their authors lack conviction in their feminist approach. So it is primarily male authors who have projected the Mennonite woman in terms of such simple categories as Eve Before the Fall and Eve After the Fall. More recent Mennonite fiction contains far more complex female characters by women authors, as well as by male authors like Rudy Wiebe and Armin Wiebe.[13]

The Mennonite women writers now in full career are anything but stereotypical in their attitudes towards women, but even when they do portray traditional Mennonite women they do so with conscious irony or compassionate understanding. What motivates most of these women writers is anger, controlled anger or, as Hildi Froese Tiessen chooses to call it in a perceptive phrase, "ambivalent lament."[14] Whether anger or ambivalent lament, these writers, like feminist writers generally, write from a new woman's perspective; they write from the margin, from the underground, "speaking the gap," in one feminist critic's phrase, between the official power language of men and the private voices or outright silence of the women. And because they were denied access to public language and self-definition, Mennonite women writers are "re-membering" themselves, articulating their experience as Mennonite women in terms of the physical experience they were privately allowed to have as wives and mothers. The boldest of them bring to the fore radical forms of expression by dramatizing their relationships with men and even with the church in starkly explicit sexual terms, sexual terms that have always been present by implication in such hallowed metaphors as "Jesus, Lover of my soul," "Christ, the bridegroom of the church," as well as in the erotic imagery of the Song of Songs.

The writer in whose work the anger bred of repression and subordination and male tyranny is at its most intense, at its most

---

[13]Ms. Wiebe might have included in her analysis, for example, Rudy Wiebe's *My Lovely Enemy* (1983), as its four female characters offer a rich diversity of characterization.

[14]Hildi Froese Tiessen, introduction to *Prairie Fire* 11 (summer 1990): 10.

dramatic and daring creatively, is the Manitoba poet Di Brandt, who arrived on the Mennonite literary scene in 1987 with a remarkable, long-delayed first volume of verse provocatively entitled *Questions i asked my mother*, which was subsequently short-listed for Canada's most prestigious literary honor, the Governor-General's Award for Poetry, and which won several other prizes. She followed this with *Agnes in the Sky* in 1990, an even more mature collection.[15] By her own admission, Brandt's motive for beginning to write poems was her life-long quarrel with her rigidly patriarchal father, a quarrel still unfinished at his death in 1979.

Di Brandt's poems are written in a deliberately low-keyed plain style in broken lines without punctuation or capitalization, often reminding the reader of a precocious child expressing its hurts and bewilderment and intuitive insights. The sensibility that controls the voice, however, is meticulous, fearless, and intense in its self-exposure and probing of intimate human relationships. In the "foreword" to her first volume she writes:

> learning to speak *in public*   to write love poems
> for all the world to read   meant betraying once &
> for all the good Mennonite daughter i tried so
> unsuccessfully to become[16]

Her impassioned quarrels over religion with her father, ranging from his literal reading of the Bible and her "questioning tone" in everything she said as a girl, to his belief in "submitting quietly to the teachings of the church," are not dramatized vindictively but with compassion, even an undertow of filial love, as in this poem describing her father in old age:

> ruling his shrunken kingdom from a wheelchair . . .
> learning gropingly to say the silent love words
> of his abdicating[17]

---

[15] Both volumes were published by Turnstone Press in Winnipeg, a non-Mennonite regional publisher that has published around twenty volumes by Mennonite authors in recent years.

[16] Di Brandt, "foreword," *Questions i asked my mother*.

[17] Ibid., 13.

And in another poem she celebrates in sensual imagery her father in his prime: "his teeth when he laughs/ are incredibly white/ the inside of his lips bright red."[18]

What probably shocked Mennonite readers most in Brandt's first volume were her six "missionary position" poems, in which she explored aspects of Mennonite faith, biblical stories, and parables entirely in terms of erotic desire and explicit love-making—the Word made flesh with a vengeance. "missionary position (1)," inspired by the familiar hymn line "Jesus, lover of my soul,"[19] is one of the most powerful and daring of these poems and I quote it in its entirety:

> let me tell you what it's like
> having God for a father & jesus
> for a lover on this old mother
> earth you who no longer know
> the old story the part about the
> Virgin being of course a myth
> made up by Catholics for an easy
> way out it's not that easy i can
> tell you right off the old man
> in his room demands bloody hard
> work he with his rod & his hard
> crooked staff well jesus he's
> different he's a good enough lay
> it's just that he prefers miracles
> to fishing & sometimes I get tired
> waiting all day for his bit of
> magic though late at night i burn
> with his fire & the old mother
> shudders and quakes under us when
> God's not looking[20]

There are several things to note about this shocking poem. Firstly, it is meant to shock, to wrench the reader violently out of his/her complacent acceptance of certain biblical metaphors without ever considering their physical and sexual implications.

---

[18]Ibid., 14.

[19]Again, I am indebted for this and other hints of interpretation in this chapter to Victor G. Doerksen's paper "'Our Father Which Art in Heaven . . .': Some Thoughts on the Father Image in Recent Mennonite Poetry," in *Acts of Concealment*, pp. 39-51.

[20]Ibid., 28.

As Brandt has said in an interview, "The bride of Christ—it is sexual imagery. But if the father and son imagery was to be taken literally, why was the feminine part just allegorical?"[21] Secondly, the reader should not remain oblivious to the humor, the sense of play in such a poem. To read it *literally* is, of course, to fall right back into the old Mennonite trap of literalism. Finally, in a strictly theological sense the poem actually presents a very conventional view of God as the stern Old Testament law giver and Christ as the New Testament radical whose message is love rather than the law.

In her new book *Agnes in the Sky*, Brandt's anger is still there but the bitterness has receded and more than one poem strikes a mature note of acceptance and reconciliation. As one reviewer has suggested, the "emotional engagement of the book is like a successful exorcism,"[22] with at least some of the poems offering "a moving expression of release from a father's—and a tradition's—violence,"[23] as in the ecstatic affirmation of life in the following lines:

> *yo!* let the rivers flow let the prairie
> grass grow let the wild rice sow its old
> magic in the wind let the God shaped
> papyrus shaped hole in our hearts disappear
> the great styrofoam wound in the sky
> weeping be healed[24]

Audrey Poetker is another young Manitoba poet whose first volume—*i sing for my dead in german*—shatters some hoary Mennonite male icons and insists fiercely on the importance and authenticity of the woman's voice. Coming as she does from a less fundamentalist-minded community than Di Brandt, Poetker writes from a more relaxed ethnic stance, without as much suppressed anger, perhaps, but with even more sexual aggressiveness, if anything. Poetker is confident and candid about her woman's role within the Mennonite ethos, but confines herself largely to explorations of her own emotional states as a lover and family rebel. She too refuses to accept the domination of fathers and grandfathers with its enforced silence of women.

[21] Di Brandt, *Mennonite Reporter*, 12 June 1989, 9.
[22] Maurice Mierau, *Prairie Fire* 11 (summer 1990): 215.
[23] Ibid., 216.
[24] Di Brandt, *Agnes in the Sky* (Winnipeg: Turnstone Press, 1990), 25.

The impossibility of meaningful communication between patriarchal father and rebellious daughter is poignantly dramatized in a poem ironically entitled "Father's Day Poem":

> half-way up the stairs
> i turn around
> dad's in the living room
> i give him the paper
>
> thank-you he says
>
> i go upstairs and cry
> into my pillow
> the feathers of grandma's chickens
> choke the sound[25]

She identifies with and tries to speak for her Low German-speaking grandmothers, whom she knows to be victims of the patriarchy. In a poem for her Gramma Poetker mourning her grandfather's death she laments:

> gramma gramma
> we got screwed
>
> i say it louder and louder
> but then knowing the rules
> leave tears to mark
> the pages
>
> of worn german songs[26]

And when she visits her dying Grandma Wiebe in the hospital, they joke and laugh together but the poet is again forced to end the poem in frustration.

> *grosmama* i say *grosmama*
> but can't remember the low german word
> for love

[25]Audrey Poetker, *i sing for my dead in german*, 17. She has also written a long powerful narrative poem about the Mennonite heritage in its historical and spiritual aspects which is, as yet, unpublished. Her second volume of verse is about to be published by Turnstone.
[26]Ibid., 13.

The point is that the word love in *Plautdietsch* is not normally used as a verb. The best one can do is say *Etj sie die goot* ("I am you good"), a linguistic aberration that may in itself be another indication of a male-dominated society.

Audrey Poetker's love poems tend to be strident, exhibitionistic, and provocative rather than tender and lyrical. The poem "so you say you love me eh" begins, "so let's pretend/ for one minute/ that you're human (no three you say/ most men last one)" and ends with the cryptic lines, "the crux of it all/ is knowing yourself to death/ my love."[27] Tender emotions and a soaring lyricism, however, suffuse the poems she wrote in memory of her grandparents and sister Susie, who were killed in a car accident, as in "touching home," an elegiac evocation of growing up with her sister:

> sprinting alongside of you
> holding back against
> the wind   letting you run
> strong   head high
> into the sweet summer . . .
> & if you won
> it was no sacrifice
> but sacrament
> in the days when you touching home
> & me touching you
> meant safe[28]

Another pair of accomplished Mennonite women poets of a rather different kind are Sarah Klassen of Winnipeg and Jean Janzen of Fresno. Both come from a Mennonite Brethren background and both write, in their different ways, from a Christian point of view within the Mennonite community. And yet, given their quiet, mature acceptance of their faith and heritage, both poets have developed richly feminine voices and perspectives as distinctive and candid as those of their more militant sister poets. They show the same serious concerns with the issues of the Mennonite woman's public presence and search for identity. Both also share Russian Mennonite family memories of the holocaust in revolutionary Russia, memories which in a sense form their starting points as poets. By way of contrast, Di

[27]Ibid., 45-46.
[28]Ibid., 65.

Brandt and Audrey Poetker are descended from the older 1870s group of Canadian Mennonites and no longer have those direct Russian memories, which may in part account for their greater sense of ethnic alienation.

In Sarah Klassen's first collection of poems—*Journey to Yalta* (1988)—the Crimean resort of Yalta functions as a *topos*, a place of the imagination whereby the poet can reflect her Russian Mennonite family past through the prism of her own impressions and emotions during a recent visit to the city. These vividly realized poems form the key section in the book and establish Klassen's voice as essentially elegiac and deceptively restrained, austere rather than mournful, compassionate and demurely open, non-confrontational but energized by a sly irony that frequently has arresting, even devastating implications. Without rejecting the patriarchal social structure, she knows how to undercut its fantasies and pretensions with a few deft images and tone to match, as in the poem "Emigrant":

> Grandfather refused to believe
> the revolution. It can't last
> he said citing God . . .
>
> Order will overcome chaos
> he assured the fugitives
> shivering in damp corners of the cold
> cellar . . .
>
> Eyes shining he reminded them, the righteous
> will inherit the land
> their enemies vanish like wind-blown smoke.
>
> Grandfather may have forgotten
> for the moment old Lazarus
> who was meek and just, and
> never gained an acre of this rich earth.[29]

Again, Sarah Klassen's imaginative identification is with the women in her family, especially her grandmother who was forced to seek a cure for her tuberculosis in Yalta in 1918, while the poet's mother, fifteen that summer, "grew restless/ having

---

[29]Sarah Klassen, *Journey to Yalta* (Winnipeg: Turnstone Press, 1988), 30.

lived too long without clapping/ her hands and dancing."[30] The patriarchal sins against women are sharply etched in poems like "Small deaths" where the Grandmother after every child lost in death, "grieving/ searched all conceivable corners/ of her soul/ for evidence of unexamined sins,"[31] and in "August, 1918" where her future mother is described as "Knowing the world/ dangles from proud words of men/ whose names you can never remember."[32] But Klassen can also be humorous in her treatment of the patriarchal imperative. She concludes a poem about her great-grandfather in Russia, who married a much younger second wife, with a wry picture:

> She walked beside him, bore him
> eight more sons. Millers and strong farmers
> they surround the old man
> sitting in honour beside her coffin.[33]

Eschewing the spirited self-dramatization of Di Brandt and Audrey Poetker, Sarah Klassen chooses instead to remain the sensitive, empathetic observer who locates her own identity by providing voices and presences for her foremothers while remaining self-possessed and keenly aware of her own heritage and where she fits into it.

Words For The Silence (1984) is the suggestive title of Jean Janzen's first book of poems. Since then her poems, both old and new, have appeared in several anthologies and in various journals. Like Sarah Klassen, Janzen finds meaning in her Russian-Mennonite past by exploring the personalities and destinies of her forebears, those who escaped the revolutionary horrors and those who were sucked into the Red vortex. She too takes as her *topos* the patriarchy in which the woman's voice remains private or harshly repressed altogether. In the poem "These Words Are For You, Grandmother," a touching tribute to a grandmother who committed suicide in unexplained circumstances, the poet imagines herself as vocal surrogate for a foremother unable to speak for herself:

[30]Ibid., 39.
[31]Ibid., 2.
[32]Ibid., 10.
[33]Ibid., 29.

The photograph tells me that I
have eyes and hands like yours
and a mouth with a heavy lower lip.
Look, I am shaping it for words,
making sounds for you. I am speaking
the syllables you couldn't say.[34]

Jean Janzen's poetic instincts are always for affirmative
interaction, for the balm of reconciliation. In "This Moonless
Night," she interweaves remembered images from a trip to the
Soviet Union with images and scenes from the cruel Russian past
in which her ancestors suffered.

These stands of birches are like music
on a page, or music itself, the delicate
branches drooping and swaying among
the straight trunks of paper-white . . .

I think of the women and children,
the grandfathers, who tried to hide
among them, how they were pushed
from cattle cars onto empty steppes
of Kazakhstan, how some survived on
field mice in their earthen huts.

But the poem ends on a fine note of spiritual harmony:

Listen to that music.
Chekhov's Masha walks among the trees.
We must live, she says. And the new
generation of birches grows whiter,
even in the moonless night.[35]

Much of Janzen's work breathes this kind of gentle hope for
humanity and expresses the quiet joy of fulfilled love and
acceptance in a modern world that has room for faith and
transcendence as well as for pain and suffering. There are
moments, she writes in "Sometimes," when "we know/ with a

---

[34]Jean Janzen, et al., *Three Mennonite Poets* (Intercourse, Penn.: Good Books, 1986), 10.
[35]Jean Janzen, *Piecework: 19 Fresno Poets*, eds. Jon Veinberg & Ernesto Trejo (Albany, California: Silver Skates Publishing, 1987), 59.

certainty/ that we are not made/ for earth/ a feeling/ that already/ with hair burning/ we rise."[36] She is a poet who knows how to uplift by interweaving elegiac past with celebratory present.

To include the widely acclaimed Sandra Birdsell among Mennonite writers may border on the presumptuous, although her mother was of Russian-Mennonite descent and Birdsell grew up in the partly Mennonite town of Morris in southern Manitoba. Her father, however, was Métis, that is, of mixed French-Canadian and Indian blood, and Birdsell claims that she does not think of herself as a Mennonite writer.[37] Growing up in a mixed family in an ethnically diverse community, she must have felt much like the teen-aged girl in one of her short stories who reflects disgustedly: "Being Mennonite was like having acne. It was shameful, dreary. No one invited you out."[38] Nevertheless, her three published volumes of fiction all include Mennonite characters, themes, and narrative situations, and her work fits well within the parameters of Mennonite writing I laid out in my opening chapter.

Birdsell's two volumes of short stories, collectively titled *Agassiz Stories*, as well as her novel *The Missing Child* (1989), have as their main setting the town of Agassiz, apparently modelled on her home town of Morris. The central characters in her short stories are members of the Lafreniere family, again modelled on her own Bartlette family. Since almost all her stories have female protagonists, the woman's point of view is all-pervasive in Birdsell's works. Beginning with Mika, the Lafreniere mother, and continuing with her (mostly) rebellious daughters, the ethnic atmosphere of the stories tends to be more Mennonite than Métis. But Mika and her daughters Betty, Lureen, and Truda feel culturally and ethnically misplaced, separated from their roots, confused and angry over their lack of identity. Trapped within a patriarchal system, low on the social ladder, and despised in town as a mixed breed of people, they defiantly seek freedom and independence. As one critic has noted, "Birdsell's characters live on the edges, uncertain of their connection with their parents

---

[36]*Three Mennonite Poets*, 29.
[37]Sandra Birdsell, *Prairie Fire* 11 (summer 1990): 191.
[38]Sandra Birdsell, *Agassiz Stories* (Winnipeg: Turnstone Press, 1987), 131.

and grandparents, their siblings, their neighbors, their friends, their society, their religion."[39] ·

Mika, the mother, is one of the most tortured souls in Birdsell's fiction. Raised to be the subservient Mennonite wife and mother, she yearns for a freer life herself while anxiously trying to protect her sexually precocious daughters from young male predators, not to mention their own hot blood. In "The Rock Garden" Mika makes a symbolic gesture of rebellion by taking the day off from cooking for her large brood and even from taking care of the babies, and spends her day in the heavy labor of making a rock garden for herself. In another story—"Night Travellers"—she has a brief fling behind her husband's back with an itinerant workman in defiance of her elderly Russian-Mennonite father, who spies on her. He appeals to her in private as a concerned father and Christian:

> "We're a community," he said. "People united by our belief, like a family. When one member hurts, the whole family suffers."
> "A family. I'm not part of a family," Mika said. "I don't belong anywhere."
> "How can you say that? The [Mennonite] women welcome you into their homes. They pray for you."
> "Oh, they welcome me alright. I'm to be pitied, prayed for. It gives them something to do."[40]

We note here that while the old Mennonite patriarch can act as the voice of conscience, he is powerless to control his daughter's conduct or, indeed, the attitudes of her family, a family "lost" to the Mennonite heritage he represents. When the same Grandfather Thiessen dies in a later story, "The Day My Grandfather Died," granddaughter Lureen, who despises her Mennonite family connections and tries to be French Canadian to the point of speaking English with a French accent, tries to avoid her hurt and grief by skipping school and spending the afternoon at the home of Claudette, her French-Canadian girlfriend. Lureen drinks beer with her friend and watches her dancing lasciviously with a young family workman. In the end she gets sick, and

[39]Charlene Diehl-Jones, "Sandra Birdsell's *Agassiz Stories*: Speaking the Gap," in *Contemporary Manitoba Writers*, ed. Kenneth James Hughes (Winnipeg: Turnstone Press, 1990), 96.
[40]Birdsell, *Agassiz Stories*, 82.

filled with self-loathing breaks down, weeping and trying to justify her grief and love for her grandfather to Claudette:

> "An old man is an old man, right? It doesn't matter what nationality, they're all the same. He was old and he was mine and he died."[41]

And so in her grief Lureen defiantly finds her woman's voice, a voice that asserts her rebellion but also accepts the humanity that binds her to family and her Mennonite heritage as well. But that is about as close as a Sandra Birdsell character can come to an open acknowledgment of ethnic identity.

Magdalene Redekop and her sister Elizabeth Falk have recently begun experimenting with a new form of feminist writing, a marvelously subtle "re-membering" of the Mennonite woman through a form of double-voiced fiction based on private memories of a shared family background. In the two two-part narratives the sisters have published so far, they develop memories and themes contrapuntally with one sister recalling private images associated with growing up in the Falk family in southern Manitoba, images which the second sister then picks up and weaves into her narrative with additions and variations of her own. The result is a rich narrative fugue that transforms private memories and feelings into unique patterns of shared insight and meaning.[42] At the centre of these meditations on the woman's neglected experience within a patriarchal Mennonite family and community is the mother of the Falk family, the matriarchal link whom Magdalene Redekop celebrated in the fine autobiographical essay to which I alluded earlier.

No brief analysis would do justice to the subtle insights and illuminating use of language in these wonderful fictional recreations by the two sisters, so a brief description of their techniques along with a few illustrations will have to suffice. In her narrative "Moving: 1. The House," Elizabeth Falk, trying to survive the painful process of a divorce, begins by reminiscing about all the places she lived in during her unhappy marriage. That leads her to reminiscing about the "the big white house" in the country that was the Falk home when the family was

---

[41]Ibid., 141.

[42]Elizabeth Falk and Magdalene Redekop, "Side by Side by," in *Canadian Literature* 127 (winter 1990): 10-28, and "Moving 1. The House" and "Moving 2. The Little Dipper," in *Prairie Fire* 11 (summer 1990): 20-45.

growing up. Personal and family memories rise up on wings of association: her grandfather supervising the building of her parents' house, sister Magdalene being conceived in the granary their parents were living in while waiting for the house to be completed, her father's stern injunction that the exact, literal truth must be told at all times, her fears that the family home would be broken into because it was never locked at night, the house filled with the laughter of eleven children, and finally the house being sold and moved to another location, its identity completely altered for her as a result. Amidst all her memories Elizabeth Falk is learning how to be an individual again: "I am alone now," she writes. "I am not afraid. My apartment is on the fourth floor and faces east. Every morning the sunrise is different."[43]

Magdalene Redekop, in her answering narrative "Moving: 2. The Little Dipper," examines her sister's images and memory associations by holding them up to her own light of memory and adding to them her own related images, making them all render more and more facets of meaning. At first Redekop expresses fear of entering the family home via memory again. She recalls instead the setting of the house, the reassuring sights and sounds and smells she associates with the old farmyard.[44] When she does enter the house in memory she is relieved to find the warm presence of her mother, who "can swell up so big that she fills up the whole house."[45] Redekop also recalls key Low German words and phrases which become leitmotifs for her memory, yielding ever richer meanings as she stops to examine them.

Redekop does not, however, insist on hard-and-fast meaning in her story, the kind demanded by autobiography or social history. At one point she says: "This is fiction . . . I see that I write fiction because I do not have the answers. All I can do is put things side by side or show how they look when they lie on top of each other.'[46] And in her concluding section she confesses,

> I can't make an end unless I admit that this is all made up from beginning to the end. This is not really family history. This is not about one family that is unlike all other families. . . . It is about how I make things up because I need

---

[43]Elizabeth Falk, "Moving 1. The House," in *Prairie Fire* 11 (summer 1990): 27.
[44]Magdalene Redekop, "Moving 2. The Little Dipper," in *Prairie Fire* 11 (summer 1990): 32-33.
[45]Ibid., 41.
[46]Ibid., 43.

to believe that I was made in the [granary]. It is about how we all need to believe that we began in love and will end in love. We need it so much that we will do almost anything to make it come out that way. Making fiction is like making love.[47]

What is of crucial significance here is the primacy of the imagination and the unique kind of language it utilizes in recovering the woman's identity. Only by revitalizing the woman's experience through the creative imagination can her voice be publicly sounded, her body made visible. Otherwise, as Redekop puts it in her earlier essay, the Mennonite woman remains "a body without a mouth."[48] The private, domestic women's stories "urgently demand to be told side by side, lovingly, because only this love prevents the body of the mother being torn apart."[49] That is the true re-membering of the Mennonite woman through the power of the imagination with its "ability to identify with another," as Redekop expresses it.[50]

And she repeatedly invokes Low German words and phrases because in her Mennonite tradition "it is the language of domesticity and laughter," and therefore preeminently suited to the woman's voice.[51] A particularly beautiful example is the way the Low German word *leljebleiv* (lavender or pale purple), her mother's favorite color, conjures up an image of an act of love and beauty for Redekop. She remembers that her farmer father always seeded flax in a field that could be seen from her parents' bedroom and surmises now that he did so because he knew how her mother adored the lavender color of flax in bloom. And so this closing memory becomes a metaphor through which the myth of patriarchal power combines with the private myth of the Mennonite woman's love for beauty and color to form a rich mythic collage of love and reconciliation.

In summary, what is impressive about Mennonite women's writing, apart from its honesty and fearlessness, is its unwillingness to accept male literary models per se, its sensitivity in letting literary forms and voices rise spontaneously from the well of creativity without trying to force them into the controlled power myths preferred by male writers. What emerges in the

---

[47]Ibid., 44.
[48]"Through the Mennonite Looking Glass," 239.
[49]Redekop, "Side by Side by," 18.
[50]Ibid.
[51]Ibid., 45.

writing of these women is a new kind of Mennonite voice, a voice that does not seek to impose order and coherence on Mennonite experience, to set up a traditional hierarchy of agreed-upon meaning, a set of disciplined, male-oriented myths supposedly defining and expressing the collective experience. Instead, women writers develop more natural, more subversive voices that are not afraid to speak their own vulnerability, their own defencelessness, their powerlessness to provide definitive and dramatic answers to the big questions of human existence. In the end, of course, the stories and poems of women writers *do* take the form of literary myths, but they are more tentative, open-ended, and unassuming literary myths, myths that will take readers into the warm intimate embrace of the experience itself, rather than attempting to penetrate and interpret the puzzling, unyielding nature of that experience. Thus, the writing of Mennonite women is bringing a new enriching dimension to the exciting phenomenon of Mennonite writing today, a dimension that for the first time acknowledges the full public identity of women in Mennonite society.[52]

I want to conclude this book by exploring the delicate often ambivalent relationship between Mennonite writers and their community, what the spiritual and ethnic implications are of a growing body of literature that is no longer speaking for and from the established center but rather from the dissident frontier from which all good art and literature speaks.

[52]Space prevented me from including in my discussion other fine women poets and writers of fiction like Lois Braun, Sara Stambaugh, Anne Konrad, Rosemary Deckert Nixon, Marjorie Toews, Dora Dueck, Raylene Hinz-Penner, and others.

Chapter 4

To Whom Are the Voices Speaking?

Writing From Outside the Inside:
Mennonite Writers and the Community

In this final chapter I want to address a provocative question: Are the new Mennonite literary prophets being listened to or spurned by the Mennonite community? Before attempting to answer that question I need to disentangle myself from a web of related questions raised by the first one. In what sense are these writers prophetic? Are they perhaps false prophets? How can they be true prophets to Mennonite readers when many of them aren't even practising Mennonites, or indeed professing Christians? And even if we think of them as prophets, are they not prophets of doom rather than prophets of hope?

Perhaps we can agree that a prophet does not necessarily have to be a messenger of God in the biblical sense, but can be someone who is gifted with a more than ordinary spiritual and moral insight, perhaps one who acts as an evangelist bringing a message of new significance to the community. A belief in the artist as divinely inspired, a bearer of the highest truths, has been supported by great thinkers and writers from Plato in antiquity to Sir Phillip Sidney in the 16th century, to Shelley in the 19th and William Butler Yeats in the 20th. Thus, in one form or another the hieratic function of art and artists has been acknowledged from time immemorial. Contemporary Mennonite artists have expressed support for the view that art is a sacred trust. Poet Patrick Friesen makes the claim: "Art is not a career to choose in the usual sense of career choice. Although not many talk like this now, art is a calling. Rooted in who or what one is from birth and circumstance. The question is what a person does with the call."[1] American-Mennonite musician Carol Weaver has said: "Our art, like our life, needs to dare speak truth: only then will it be Anabaptist. . . . Perhaps our best preaching, prophesying, healing can be done through art. Then art is *highly* Anabaptist!"[2] And Menno Wiebe, a Winnipeg poet and MCC director, has written: "[T]he modern outburst of art is in a 'lay' expression of Mennonites. It reflects a thumping kind of theology which cannot be monopolized by the official, and increasingly

---

[1]Patrick Friesen, in *Prairie Fire* 11 (summer 1990): 164.
[2]Carol Weaver, in *Festival Quarterly* (August September October 1976): 10.

professional clergy. Thus, we see in the expression of art, a rebirth of the priesthood of all believers."[3]

Whether or not we fully endorse these claims, they do tell us that art, including our literature, should be taken seriously and may be offering us something of vital importance for our spiritual well-being and cultural health. We may not always like the non-conformity, the stubborn independence, the sheer ego-driven impudence of the artist, but we should avoid the temptation of naively confusing his/her personality, personal attitudes, and way of life with the art produced by the inspired artist. After all, even the Old Testament prophets, those chosen instruments of God, were notoriously self-willed and often intractable to the point of flagrant disobedience.

We should not forget that Mennonite writers are writing with the weight of almost five centuries of Anabaptist-Mennonite faith, doctrine, and practise, as well as ethnic culture resting on their shoulders. For many of them that accumulated weight has become mostly dead weight that stultifies the imagination and deadens the soul. They know that we Mennonites have tried to shelter ourselves from the sinful world by isolating ourselves. And that our isolation has bred its own strains of sin—from false humility to a subtle sense of pride in our own superiority. We have always found it easier to point to the sins of those outside than to the sins within us. Our officially sanctioned history is largely one of self-righteousness and pharisaical self-congratulation. Only now are we beginning to question our triumphalist view of our own history and achievements and taking a more critical look at ourselves. We desperately need artists who have wrestled long and hard with evil—both outside and inside of themselves—and who are committed to exposing our spiritual hypocrisies, our shallow moralism, our incessant but often aimless church activities. The creative artist also knows that out of evil can come good. At the very least we need our dissident writers as prophetic warning voices.

We should not, however, expect our writers to be fire-and-brimstone preachers. Facile didacticism is not the method of the true artist. Rudy Wiebe had to learn early in his career as a novelist that if you want to be a creative moralist, to write with a serious vision, you had better not resort to naked didacticism if you want morally literate readers to accept you. Our better writers today are *interpreters* of Mennonite experience rather than

[3] Ibid., 11.

mere *reflectors* or *advocates* of it, and that means they must write from a free, open frontier removed from the center where the received meaning has been sanctioned, where the accepted ideology is considered as complete and self-sufficient. Writing from outside the inside means resisting the pull of the establishment center while maintaining vital contact with it. And that is no easy feat. Hildi Froese Tiessen describes many Mennonite writers today as "occupying the discomforting gap between belief and superstition, between the coherence of an ethos where vision and purpose and faith sustain meaning and the fragmentation of a world where social and religious dogmas loom merely as abandoned monuments in a landscape of forgotten ceremonies."[4]

There is always a danger, of course, that the prophetic voice at its most persuasive and insistent may bring about a self-fulfilling prophecy. The voices of most Mennonite writers are meant to be heard not only within the community but well beyond it. When our better writers shake up our spiritual complacency, challenge our cultural stereotypes, subvert our middle-class pretensions, and discredit our accumulated false myths, they achieve, at their best, literary universals that resonate for readers everywhere. In reaching for those universals, however, Mennonite writers may ultimately be denying their separateness, the uniqueness of their Mennonite experience, and themselves contributing to the already ongoing disintegration of ethnic identity.

As Patrick Friesen suggested at the 1990 Mennonite writers' conference at Conrad Grebel College, the mirror that Mennonite writers hold up to the Mennonite community to see what we look like can just as easily become a window through which we are shown the outside world from the perspective of our own experience. In an interview several years ago, Di Brandt put it more bluntly: "I think that literature is one of the ways of destroying [Mennonite] separateness . . . I'm helping to kill it off."[5] And if this is indeed what is happening, should we be honoring the literary prophets who are helping to bring about our ethnic demise, or ostracize them as Cassandras we don't want to hear? The question is a troubling one and admits of no easy answers.

[4]Hildi Froese Tiessen, introduction to *Prairie Fire* 11 (summer 1990): 10.
[5]Maurice Mierau, "Rebel Mennos Move into the Arts," *Midcontinental* (Midwinter 1987-88): 19.

So far I have been sketching a picture of the Mennonite artist as outsider-prophet, one who insists on bringing new knowledge into the community about itself, an iconoclast of the imagination who smashes illusions and self-deceptions regardless of group solidarity or collective self-esteem. That is the kind of Mennonite writer who is in the ascendancy today. There is, admittedly, another entirely different way of looking at the Mennonite writer and her function vis-a-vis the community. And that is the kind of creative approach advocated so persuasively by John L. Ruth in *Mennonite Identity and Literary Art*. What he called for was a Mennonite art and literature created by artists who would accept the full burden of the Mennonite story and heritage, and "speak from a center of conviction and commitment to that heritage."[6] Ruth was most emphatically not calling for mere literary apologists or religious propagandists for the Mennonite cause. The Mennonite artist, he argued, should be free within reasonable limits to criticize his people, to touch upon the "negative distortions" of his heritage, but not at the expense of denying or obscuring the essential "salvation story" of the Anabaptist-Mennonite tradition. Ruth voiced his own artistic credo with deep conviction:

> To achieve a creative balance between critique and advocacy . . . to be a whole person, and then to speak from the core of a tradition which gave me the priceless gift of identification with the kingdom of God—these are the desires by which I . . . am driven as I consider attempting the art of fiction.[7]

And that is the kind of writing John Ruth himself and a few others, like the poet Jeff Gundy and novelists like Merle Good, Sara Stambaugh, and Levi Miller, have been doing in the Swiss-Mennonite tradition. However, as I have demonstrated at length in earlier chapters, the kind of community-centered, committed Christian writing Ruth called for is not what we are getting from Mennonite writers in the Russian-Mennonite tradition. We might do well to ask ourselves why not.

I pointed out earlier that in the latter tradition there was an emphasis on individualism going back to Russia and

---

[6]John L. Ruth, *Mennonite Identity and Literary Art* (Scottdale: Herald Press, 1978), 65.

[7]Ibid., 63.

strengthened in Canada through the influence of North American fundamentalism and more recently through acculturation and urbanization among Mennonites of Dutch-Russian background. John Ruth points out that Dutch Mennonites from the 17th century onwards were much more individualisticly minded and hence much more inclined to enter the arts than were the considerably more conservative and communally minded Swiss Mennonites. The latter, according to Ruth, saw the worldly involvement of their northern coreligionists "as a barometer of a sinking of their spiritual fervor, a symptom of acculturation and abandonment of key elements of their covenant soul."[8] Whether or not there was a loss of spiritual fervor among the Dutch Mennonites, their tendency towards cultural secularization is indisputable, and existed among the Mennonites of Russia as well in later times.

An emphasis on individualism and secular culture is much more likely to lead to the kind of art and writing we have been getting from artists in the Dutch-Russian-Canadian tradition than to the kind advocated by John Ruth for the more community-centered, inward-looking Swiss Mennonites. What Ruth regards as the desired norm is essentially an orally inspired version of the Mennonite story which reflects the collective experience and wisdom and faith of a people, individual stories harmonized and patterned to accommodate and form one master story: "A Story over-arching these stories," in his words.[9] And his model, of course, is the Bible. The oral tradition calls for group participation and interaction, the insider talking to other insiders within the community about shared experiences, collective understanding and wisdom adding up to a totality of what the community knows and values.

Modern Western written literature, however, has developed in a direction away from the community as the repository of accumulated meaning and wisdom. The literate artist is by nature and calling an outsider, even when he is positioned and privileged to be an insider of his group. His calling is to penetrate to the individual heart of the matter—"the heart of darkness"—to lead the advance, to be the scout and preliminary mapmaker of that part of the interior landscape of the mind and soul not yet fully explored or charted. An oral tradition implies subordination of the individual ego to the group consciousness

[8]Ibid., 31.
[9]Ibid., 20.

and will, a written tradition implies an individual ego at odds with the group mentality in important ways as a critic, prober, exposer, and indeed celebrator, but never in subordination to the collective will and consciousness. Patrick Friesen asserts the complete autonomy of the artist in no uncertain terms: "There is no authority over art. Not religious, not social, nor political, not academic, not theoretical."[10]

John Ruth identifies the "classic issues" of our Mennonite ethos as "obedience, simplicity, humility, defenselessness, the questioning of progress, the maintenance of identity," and implies that they have not received "an aesthetically serious representation" in our literature.[11] One can agree that these "issues" have not been the focus of much Mennonite writing in either tradition. The question is, could they ever be? Jeff Gundy, in a bold and interesting article, has isolated one of these issues—"humility"—and applied it to Mennonite literary works as a kind of litmus test. In the process, he finds current Mennonite literature, especially in the Russian-Canadian tradition, somewhat lacking. Yet for all its vigor and ingeniousness, Gundy's analysis strikes me as a bit one-sided and overzealous, although in fairness I must add that he is cognizant of the essential differences between the Swiss-Mennonite and Russian-Mennonite approaches to literature and willing to make at least some allowances for them.

But not enough, in my opinion. When he describes critic Hildi Froese Tiessen as having an "almost exclusively aesthetic understanding of Mennonite art and literature,"[12] he fails to do justice either to her understanding of Russian-Canadian Mennonite literature or to that literary tradition itself. And his charge that Canadian-Mennonite critics and writers "have developed a straightforward willingness to celebrate their own successes"[13] ignores the fact that Canadian-Mennonite literature is emerging within the larger context of Canadian literature, has indeed become an integral part of it, and could not hope to remain anonymous and unheralded even if it wanted to.

No reasonable person would deny Gundy's "underlying assumption . . . that no artist is truly an isolated individual. Whatever the particular relation to the community, both artists

---

[10]Patrick Friesen, *Prairie Fire* 11 (summer 1990): 164.
[11]Ruth, 23.
[12]Jeff Gundy, "Humility in Mennonite Literature," *Mennonite Quarterly Review* 63 (January 1989): 9.
[13]Ibid., 13.

and their works are inevitably and complexly linked to their social and physical environment."[14] But that symbiotic relationship does not limit the writer's function to that of humble ideologue for the community. Humility may be a valid Mennonite theme but hardly a touchstone for Mennonite writing.[15] Shirley Hershey Showalter, in her thoughtful and gracefully written "Response" to Jeff Gundy's article on humility, makes the telling point that humility works best in literature when it is freely chosen by the author, and not imposed from without.[16] And that takes us back to the all-important issue of the artist's autonomy, his/her freedom to create without the restraints of an imposed ideology.

The theory so convincingly developed by John Ruth as a desideratum for Mennonite literary art has not, on the whole, been borne out in practise. If anything, there is a growing discrepancy between his theory and what in fact is happening in Mennonite art and literature. It may be that the creative balance between "critique and advocacy" is too difficult for today's Mennonite writers to achieve even if they wanted to, and clearly most of them do not want to write within the community "scruples" so clearly defined by Ruth. "To *wrestle through* the issues in the artist's personal encounter with a special tradition," he writes, "that is the challenge."[17] Precisely, but how can the artist do that fully and honestly without facing the possibility that after wrestling through the issues she may find herself in fundamental disagreement with the prevailing ideology of the community. That is a chance the artist of integrity must take, and that means exercising autonomy as an artist, to be free of even the most reasonable or cherished "scruples" in his/her tradition. The true artist is a Jacob fearlessly wrestling the angel and in the end prevailing. He is not a Jacob carefully setting the rules of the

---

[14]Ibid., 11.

[15]When Gundy argues, for example, that Armin Wiebe's Yasch Siemens' being integrated into his community is an example of the "humility tradition" existing among Canadian Mennonites (p.17), he is mistaking humility for the *conformity* of Yasch that this comic novel insists on and missing the irony of the "happy" Mennonite ending, that is, Yasch gaining the status that allows him to fit comfortably into his religio-ethnic Mennonite community.

[16]Shirley Hershey Showalter, "Bringing the Muse Into Our Country: A Response to Jeff Gundy's 'Humility in Mennonite Literature,'" *Mennonite Quarterly Review* 63 (January 1989): 27.

[17]Ruth, 43.

wrestling match in advance in the hope of besting the angel on the artist's own ground.

It seems significant that neither John Ruth nor Jeff Gundy ever refers to the artist's role as prophet-teacher. To do so would be to concede that the artist has access to insights and forms of knowledge that do not necessarily come from the collective experience and communal wisdom sanctioned by the community. What the artist creates should come from the power of his imagination and be guided only by his sense of artistic integrity, that is, the degree of personal commitment he is prepared to make, the extent to which he is willing to accept or reject the values of the community. The artist's sensitive antennae will tell him/her what is really happening in the community behind the thick walls of conformity and shades of self-deception. My sense is that the Mennonite writing we have been getting in recent years does reflect in the deepest sense what is actually happening in the Mennonite community, and not what we like to think is happening or hope is happening.

Peter Erb, a Canadian Swiss-Mennonite critic, has argued in a recent article that it is probably their strong belief in humility which has *prevented* the Swiss Mennonites from developing their own written literature. As Erb says, "Humility is a difficult virtue to praise. Press the point too strongly and it becomes pride, destructive of itself; attack the vice of pride in its concrete form too boldly and the result is the production of an equally haughty opposite."[18] And so Swiss Mennonites have remained content with a largely oral culture, for as Erb expresses it, "Orality always knows itself as dying. . . . It cannot gain immortality in the permanence and expansive possibilities of print. So deep does orality reside in Deitsch culture . . . that even when it is embedded in letters, the theme of oral culture remains strong."[19]

Whatever differences there are, however, between Swiss-Mennonite and Russian-Mennonite cultures, I would argue that Swiss-Mennonite writers like John Ruth, Jeff Gundy, Merle Good, Sara Stambaugh, and a few others whose work I know do not have creative sensibilities or literary aims significantly different from those of Mennonite writers in Canada. Their antennae are as fine, their insights as searching, their criticisms as valid, their literary techniques as sophisticated as those of Rudy Wiebe and company in the Russian-Mennonite tradition. What all these

---

[18]Peter Erb, *The New Quarterly* 19 (Spring/Summer 1990): 62.
[19]Ibid., 57.

writers share in abundance is the talent, commitment, honesty, and courage which characterize the serious writer in any tradition. The ultimate test is whether a writer is good enough to deserve a worthy readership, that is, readers who want good writing and will respond to it. Ultimately, it is the reader who sets the writer free, who completes the writer and justifies the writer's act of egoism, his assertion of independence in daring to expose his ideas, feelings and values for all the world to see. The literary voice has to be heard in the community, or else it remains stifled within the author's ego.

And that brings me, finally, back to the question I began with: Are the new Mennonite literary prophets being listened to or ignored and even spurned by the Mennonite community? Earlier Mennonite writers wrote in German, almost exclusively for Mennonite readers even when the writers were, like Arnold Dyck and his generation, Mennonites largely in an ethnocultural sense. It followed that their readership was homogeneous, undemanding, and small. Arnold Dyck complained that in the thirties and forties he could never get beyond a readership of around 600 in Canada, and as a consequence he had to keep his books down to about 100 pages in length so that by selling them at a dollar a copy he could at least recover printing costs.[20] Those readers expected and usually got nostalgic stories and poems about their lost Russian homeland, or else gently comic stories and sketches in which they and their kind tried to understand an often baffling new North American society and culture. The rest of the books were either amateurish novels about the Russian Revolution and its aftermath, depicting experiences most of the readers had shared,[21] or devotional books which made few intellectual demands on the reader and complacently fed his cultural presuppositions and spiritual beliefs.

Today's Mennonite writers have a much less clearly defined relationship with their Mennonite readers, where they can attract them at all. Indeed, most Mennonite writers confront a sort of two-tiered readership. The lower tier consists of or at least is dominated by those readers who still want only a safe, didactic

[20]Arnold Dyck, "Aus Meinem Leben," in *Collected Works of Arnold Dyck*, vol.I, ed. Victor G. Doerksen and Harry Loewen (Winnipeg: Manitoba Mennonite Historical Society, 1985), 508.

[21]I am thinking of such novels as Gerhard Toews' *Die Heimat in Flammen* (1933) and *Heimat in Trümmern* (1936) and Peter J. Klassen's *Heimat einmal* (n.d.) and *Als die Heimat zur Fremde geworden*, as well as others.

Christian literature devoid of challenge or any view of the world as it actually exists. Here is an excerpt from a letter written by a church librarian who had ordered a copy of the anthology of contemporary Mennonite writing published as a special issue of the Manitoba literary journal *Prairie Fire* and made available at the Mennonite World Conference in Winnipeg in 1990. The lady wrote:

> The first selections I read gave me the impression that the authors were confused, maybe even out of touch with reality. But the content got progressively more objectionable. Mennonite? What qualifies an author to claim to be a Mennonite author? Birth? Heritage? Rejection of culture and moral values? Faith? Lack of faith? Granted there may be healing in purging mind and soul by the writing of unpleasant memories and experiences but such purgings should not be dumped on the reader in the name of Mennonite literature. Why the total absence of literature by Mennonite authors who would have written to the theme of the Conference? ["Witnessing to Christ in Today's World"][22]

There would seem to be a well-nigh unbridgeable gulf between readers such as this and the kind of writing we are getting from our serious writers. In other words, the Mennonite readers most in need of the explorative, visionary Mennonite writing being done today are the least likely even to allow those voices to reach them, let alone influence them.

In the upper tier of Mennonite readers are the more sophisticated who already read popular and serious literature as a matter of course and who must be won over, in many cases, from the non-Mennonite authors who set their literary standards for them. Many of these readers are interested in Mennonite writing for its own sake, but they also demand literary merit. This is one of the reasons why the more successful writers of Mennonite background are no longer writing for a specific Mennonite readership but simply for a general readership. And so the yawning cultural chasm between the cultural elite of Mennonite society (in Canada mainly urban) and the culturally conservative, still largely rural Mennonite community is not likely to be bridged in the near future by Mennonite literature and art.

[22]Letter by Elizabeth Abrahams in *Prairie Fire* 11 (winter 1990-91): 120.

The thirty-year writing career of Rudy Wiebe is marked by the often strained relations between a brilliant artist and a Mennonite community suspicious of his motives and willing to accuse him of betrayal from the outset. And his ambivalent relationship with Mennonite readers continues to this day, with the result that he still does not enjoy a secure status within the Mennonite community as a writer. From the beginning he has been vilified, ostracized, branded as a heretic, and cruelly misinterpreted by Mennonites who often did not even bother reading his novels. The very readers who had most to gain from his ground-breaking first novel *Peace Shall Destroy Many* were the first to turn against him in a tide of hysterical vituperation that forced him to resign as editor of the *Mennonite Brethren Herald* in the early sixties. He was called everything from Devil Incarnate to—in rural Manitoba the crowning insult then—a dirty "communist."

Of course that experience, painful though it was, was the best thing that ever happened to Rudy Wiebe the writer. It was the making of him as an artist who had nothing further to lose in the Mennonite community, who was now free to develop his potential knowing that the worst had already happened to him. In his 1987 Marjorie Ward lecture at St. John's College, Winnipeg, Wiebe told the story of that traumatic experience at the outset of his novelistic career with wit, tolerance, and considerable insight. He described how the guardians of Mennonite moral and spiritual purity attacked him in letters. A minister from Snowflake, Manitoba, almost hyperventilated with fury:

> [W]hat prompted you to write as you did [?] [everything] portrayed in the negative sense, backward, isolationist, language barrier, and outwardly a pacifist, but underneath beware! [. . .] and the level to which you reduce the women is scandalous, portrayed as pure animalism [!], I'm sure that the same subject gets better treatment in "shunt literature" [junk literature][23]

Not all the letters and responses he received, however, were condemnatory, Wiebe reported, especially the many approving letters from women.

[23]Rudy Wiebe, "The Skull in the Swamp," *Journal of Mennonite Studies* 5 (1987): 16.

Rudy Wiebe has not published a novel since 1983, his longest hiatus ever, and one wonders why. Is it because his most recent novel *My Lovely Enemy* again elicited a stormy reception not only among Mennonite readers but from the Mennonite Brethren church hierarchy, dealing as the novel did with the subject of adulterous love among other controversial themes? I said in my analysis of *My Lovely Enemy* that I regard it as "a profoundly Christian work of almost unbearable intensity" which makes splendid use of post-modern and magic realism techniques. That is not how it was perceived, for the most part, in the Canadian Mennonite community. Many Mennonite readers, including church officials, insisted on reading it as a realistic novel gone bad, that is, gone bad in the sense of being "pornographic" in its vivid portrayal of love-making, as well as in the sense of justifying the adulterous love affair between James Dyck and Gillian Overton (not to mention the allegedly blasphemous "interviews" Professor Dyck had with Jesus).

What drew a particularly vehement response was a somewhat mixed but largely favorable and supportive review of *My Lovely Enemy* in *Mennonite Brethren Herald*, the conference magazine from which, ironically, Wiebe had been forced to resign as editor back in 1962. In a 1984 newspaper interview, the then moderator of the MB conference expressed his two main concerns with the novel as being the implication in it "that Jesus had a sex life and that it had not dealt conclusively with the topic of adultery, treating it as a reasonable option."[24] Again we find here the old Mennonite habit of reading fiction as though it were a form of discursive writing like history or theology. Even the review in the *Herald* closed with a plea of tolerance for a talented "brother" who did not always get things right ideologically. To its everlasting credit, however, Wiebe's home church in Edmonton, the Lendrum congregation, held a public celebration in honor of the author and his novel.

Not surprisingly, Rudy Wiebe has become somewhat disillusioned with Mennonite readers. More and more he has been aiming his fiction at a general readership while continuing to hope that his Mennonite readers will learn to read his work as fiction and give him the respect he deserves as a major literary artist. In a perceptive and cogently argued article—"The Naming of Rudy Wiebe"—Canadian-Mennonite critic Paul Tiessen shows

[24]John Redekop, in an interview in the *Kitchener-Waterloo Record*, 2 June 1984.

that in some of Wiebe's recent short stories and essays he is dramatizing his own narrative voice in ways that are clearly autobiographical and in which he seems to be trying to educate his readers in the admittedly difficult art of how to read Rudy Wiebe, the fiction-writing visionary Christian, moralist, and satirist. As Tiessen says, "Wiebe's method [in these recent works] implies that his greatness as a writer is predicated upon a greatness which he must find, even create, within the reader."[25] Needless to say, that is a daunting task for any writer, especially one whose expressed aim has always been to make a better world through his fiction, and one can only hope that Rudy Wiebe will gradually succeed in attracting the readers, both Mennonite and non-Mennonite, that his complex and visionary works deserve.

Apart from such controversial themes as sex, religious hypocrisy, criticism of the church, and the like, nothing arouses the ire of conservative Mennonite readers more than what they regard as unacceptable language in much of the Mennonite writing we are getting nowadays. Indeed, this may be a sensitive issue even for more sophisticated Mennonite readers, but it is one that needs to be faced squarely if Mennonite writers are to be taken seriously as prophetic voices for the Mennonite community. That the shibboleth of "acceptable" language exists is not surprising. It is, after all, based on the Mennonite tradition of plain speech: the biblical "let your yea be yea, and your nay, nay," neither more nor less than the truth, and no "swearing" in either sense of that word. Unfortunately, that is not how people nowadays express themselves, not even most Mennonites, and good literature is, after all, written in the language—the idioms and expressions—that people actually use. All too often the bias against the use of so-called "coarse" language in literary writing turns out to be another attempt to control and coerce the writer into a style that conforms to the censor's notion of what is acceptable language rather than the writer's. The notion that there is "good" language and "bad" language per se is itself demonstrably false and misguided. To demand a sterilized literary language purged of all imputed verbal dross is to force the serious writer to rely on a crippled vocabulary, to distort not only his style but to falsify characterization, theme, and tone as well.

[25]Paul Tiessen, "The Naming of Rudy Wiebe," *Journal of Mennonite Studies* 7 (1989): 118.

In talking some years ago to a senior editor from Herald Press about the Mennonite historical novel I was then working on, I was warned about the use of "coarse" language and that Herald Press would have none of it. Any good writer, he informed me, could avoid objectionable language in a given narrative situation by simply writing around it. I am sure he was right about the technical problem, but I am less sure about his artistic assumptions. A publishing house has the right to impose any form of censorship on its writers that its readers are willing to accept or demand. The writer who complies with this form of stylistic censorship, however, will need to search his/her conscience to determine whether artistic integrity has been violated. When conservative readers ask me why I used coarse language in my novel *My Harp is Turned to Mourning* my tongue-in-cheek answer is that only the bad characters in my novel use that kind of language. But the issue is clear. I did not want Russian terrorists and murderous peasants to sound like Mennonites when they hadn't talked that way in real life. I wanted my Mennonite characters to sound life-like by not using swear words, and I wanted my Russian characters to sound life-like by swearing like Russians. And I certainly did consider artistic integrity to be my guiding principle in that.

Yeats' Crazy Jane says to the self-righteous Bishop in the poem: "Fair and foul are near of kin,/ and fair needs foul. . . ." Fair and foul imply each other, and that is nowhere more true than in literature. The defiant children's taunt "Sticks and stones will break my bones but words will never hurt me," may be self-delusion in real life, but the claim that words will never hurt you is perfectly true in literature. In literature *all* language used with artistic integrity can only help us, help us to understand ourselves and each other better. Call coarse language the devil's language if you like, but good writers use it as necessary ballast for the more ethereal forms of language that without it can lead to sentimentality. They need it to strike sparks of verbal energy available in no other way. Even the taboo four-letter words (that every child knows by the time it starts school) should be available to a good writer for artistic purposes. Like other artists, writers have different sensibilities and different ways of dramatizing and expressing human experience in art. But they should never feel inhibited by social language taboos from doing what their artistic instincts tell them to do. All the resources of language should be available to verbal artists at all times, subject only to the limits of their creative imaginations and powers of expression. As for Mennonite readers, they will need to overcome whatever socially conditioned prejudices they have about some forms of language if they wish to move fully into the exciting new world of Mennonite literature. Many Mennonite readers, I suspect, are fearful of having their delicate sensibilities bruised by what they consider to be offensive language, to have their pet prejudices derided, their false pieties exposed, when that is exactly what the author is trying to do. To ruffle feathers, to rub the wrong way through the creative use of language is what serious literature is all about, and particularly Mennonite literature at this moment in our history. The responsible artist, burning with a secret passion, tries to find a way through the briars of prejudice and insecurity so that he can awaken us to the truth and beauty of real life and leave behind the deceptive fantasies, the expedient dreams, the self-incriminating nightmares.

What does the future hold for Mennonite writing? I wish I knew. As I see it, Mennonite writers are at the moment in a bit of a dilemma, almost a Catch-22 situation as far as their relations with the Mennonite community are concerned. On the one hand they are intensely engaged in a family dialogue—some would say family quarrel—with the community as they continue to challenge its religious traditions and long-accepted prejudices and practises, its pressures to conform, its ethnic complacency, and a whole host of other issues that need airing by serious writers. In so doing, however, Mennonite writers often antagonize beyond reconciliation the very readers they hope to reach and influence. On the other hand, the Mennonite establishment, including the church, is now, at least in some places, liberal enough and astute enough to appreciate the new attitudes and insights expressed by our better writers and would like to incorporate them into an enlarged, updated Mennonite ideology. Much as they would like to be read and accepted by Mennonite readers, however, Mennonite writers are not about to give up their independence and integrity as artists by allowing themselves to be enlisted in the cause of the liberal establishment.

There are ways, however, in which the church could give a forum to our serious writers without demanding that they become conforming members of the establishment. Our numerous church papers and magazines are filled with the multifarious activities of congregations and conferences, but how many of them ever devote space to Mennonite literary works such as new poems and fiction? With the notable exception of *Festival Quarterly* in the U.S. and the *Mennonite Reporter* and the *Mennonite Mirror* in Canada, almost no Mennonite publications have paid the slightest attention to serious Mennonite writing. In a recent letter published in the *Reporter*, poet Di Brandt asks why Mennonite publications do not make it possible for Mennonite writers "to discover our voices and appear in print? Why did almost every Mennonite writer in my generation have to make a traumatic break with the Mennonite church in order to write?"[26] Not all Mennonite writers would agree with that dramatic accusation, but almost all of them have experienced indifference and rejection in their own communities, have discovered how hard it is to get published under Mennonite auspices, and have been forced to turn elsewhere. One honorable exception to this was *Mennonite Mirror*, which in its twenty years of publication (1961-1991) made a valuable contribution to Canadian-Mennonite writing by publishing some of the early and more mature work of a number of Mennonite writers of growing reputation. Generally speaking, however, Mennonite publications have a lamentable record in this area, and the growing recognition given to Mennonite writing is coming increasingly from non-Mennonite sources, as already indicated.

In Canada, particularly in Manitoba, Mennonite writers, aware of their ambiguous status within the community, seek reinforcement from each other by forming their own close-knit writers' family within the larger tribe of Canadian writers. But that should not be taken as indicating a siege mentality. Clannishness and tribalism come naturally to writers; since writing itself is such a solitary pursuit, writers need to come out of their individual caves and seek interaction with their colleagues around a communal campfire occasionally, especially at night. Professionally, they attend writers' conferences together, support writers' organizations, participate jointly in creative writing courses and workshops, and give frequent public readings together. What is impressive about this Mennonite writers' family is its diverse character, including as it does writers who are practising Mennonites as well as the strongly dissident writers who no longer lay claim to the Mennonite community. The esprit de corps among these writers is strong.

With these various Mennonite writers influencing and cross-fertilizing each other, a canon of Mennonite literature is rapidly taking shape, its most recent impetus coming from the four anthologies of Mennonite writing published in Canada in the

[26]*Mennonite Reporter*, 21 (2 September 1991): 9.

past two years.[27] There is of course always the danger that these writers will become too clannish and inward-looking and by imitating each other lose the uniqueness of their individual voices in a chorus that is too artfully blended together. So far that does not seem to be happening and one can only hope it won't in future. As I have said, Canadian Mennonite writers are increasingly aware of themselves as also belonging to the much larger tribe of Canadian writers. A curious result of this double identity is that those who began modestly as "Mennonite" writers writing for a Mennonite readership have widened their horizons considerably, while those writers who had left their Mennonite background behind have been moving closer to the Mennonite orbit as Mennonite writing has gained attention and respectability within the Canadian literary establishment.

As for the future, I am no longer as pessimistic about Mennonite authors writing themselves out of their Mennonite experience and thus bringing about the demise of Mennonite literature as I used to be. As Northrop Frye said, it is literature that begets literature, and Mennonite literature, in Canada at least, seems to be firmly enough established to perpetuate itself indefinitely. Having developed its own ethos, categories, and characteristics, it may well continue to flourish even as the Mennonite sub-culture which has nurtured it up to now continues to erode. Sarah Klassen expresses her hope for the future of Mennonite writing in Canada in these terms:

> I don't know how quickly or how completely we will write ourselves out of the Mennonite story and become indistinguishable from the general stream of Canadian

---

[27]The anthologies, all edited or guest-edited by Hildi Froese Tiessen of Conrad Grebel College, are: *Liars and Rascals: Mennonite Short Stories* (Waterloo: University of Waterloo Press, 1989); *The New Quarterly* Special Issue: Mennonite/s Writing in Canada 10 (Spring/Summer 1990); and *Prairie Fire* A Special Issue on Canadian Mennonite Writing 11 (summer 1990). An even more recent special publication, again guest-edited by Hildi Froese Tiessen, is "A Special Issue on Patrick Friesen" of the Manitoba literary magazine *Prairie Fire* 13 (spring 1992). Besides containing some of the poet's latest work, this special issue includes a host of interviews and articles with and about Friesen by both Mennonite and non-Mennonite writers and critics. A fourth anthology, *Acts of Concealment: Mennonite/s Writing in Canada*, edited by Hildi Froese Tiessen and Peter Hinchcliffe (Waterloo, Ontario: University of Waterloo Press, 1992), includes the various proceedings—lectures, readings of new work, and a closing panel discussion on Mennonite literature—of a 1990 conference on Mennonite writing.

writing. The current fascination with *Mennonite* will pass, I suspect, while the appreciation for good *writing* will not. Whatever the content of my writing, I would want to work at it with integrity and humour and a concern for truth. No ethnic, regional or national group has a monopoly on those qualities.[28]

Surely that is the real point—not just "Mennonite" writing but "good" writing. And if some of that good writing continues to be done by writers who claim the Mennonite heritage as their own, so much the better. And if more and more Mennonite readers as well as others will read that good literature, so much the better still.

[28]Sarah Klassen, in *Prairie Fire* 11 (summer 1990): 109.

Index